I dedicate this book to my children and my nine beautiful grandchildren:
Jolie, Christie, Eleanor, Joshua, Abbie, Katie, Bethany, Joseph and Milly.
My family.
My world.

PREFACE

This book is based on a memoir written by Joan Leech (nee Burns) and developed by her daughter, Julie McGowan, using her own memories and stories her mother told her. Some names and details have been changed.

Edited by Michael McGeary and Anne McGeary Carvell. With thanks to Rebecca Bevington for additional editing.

Married to the Man Who Washed Himself Away

A memoir of motherhood, marriage and obsessive behaviour

Joan Leech

mcgeary media

McGeary Media

CONTENTS

1

THE FIRST SNOWS

The first time I met the love of my life I could have cheerfully throttled him. It was winter 1953 and the boys and girls were holding a delightfully wicked snowball fight across the iron gate that separated our playgrounds at Lawson Street School, Middlesbrough. The air was full of children's shrieks and laughter as handfuls of snow burst into clouds of fluffy white, sending us scattering in different directions as we wiped flakes out of our eyes. I was good at this game, easily dodging the boys' clumsily-aimed throws and flinging fistfuls back without a pause.

The teacher's whistle signalled the end of lunchtime break but we were having so much fun we didn't pay attention the first time, and it blew two or three more times before we finally brought an end to the match. Just as we were making muttered truces with the boys over the way, an object came hurtling through the gate and smacked me full in the face – a final snowball with a stone concealed inside. I was furious. I glared at the gaggle of boys being herded inside but I couldn't tell which of them had thrown it.

'Joan!' shouted my teacher impatiently, summoning me inside.

I rubbed the side of my face where the ice had hit me and went to the girls' toilets to determine the damage – my cheek had turned a fetching shade of beetroot red. I couldn't stop thinking about it for the entire afternoon. What a nasty thing to do!

As soon as the bell rang for the end of the day I threw on my winter coat and rushed outside to wait by the boys' entrance, plotting how I would have my revenge. A sheepish-looking boy emerged from the crowd and came over to the gate to speak to me – shuffling through the snow, which had turned to an unpleasant grey sludge covering the playground. As the culprit came closer I entertained the thought of scooping up a fistful of slush and lobbing it at him. Instead, I gave him a piece of my mind – thoroughly lacing into him. But to my surprise, he was so sweet and apologetic that in the end I just had to forgive him.

Byron was a tall, dark-haired young man of thirteen – just a few months older than me. The snowball incident forged a friendship between us that blossomed into courtship by the time the snow had melted away into the smoggy springtime air. After school we would go home for tea, change our clothes, then meet up with the other kids from various parts of North Ormesby and Cargo Fleet. I was allowed to stay out until nine o'clock on the long summer evenings, but as the freezing winter settled in and the nights drew out my curfew was cut to seven. I was under strict instructions that if I was even one minute late I would be in bother. Mam would stand and wait for me on the front doorstep, looking up the street towards the Trinity Church clock, which chimed on the hour. Most nights I would hear the bells begin to ring before I'd even started to think about coming home. Fortunately, I was a fast runner – but I often couldn't speak for panting by the time I reached our front door.

Of course, Mam didn't know I was seeing Byron at first. She would have been furious if she'd realised I was hanging out with a boy at that age, so I told her I was with my friend, Anne James, instead. By the time I turned fourteen the following year, I was getting braver and thought I'd test the boundaries by asking Mam if I could invite Byron over to ours for tea. She agreed, and after that I officially had her permission to court him.

We would meet up on the corner of South Bank Road and Cargo Fleet Lane and walk around the streets hand in hand, peering into shop windows and picking out the beautiful clothes and jewellery we'd buy if we had all the money in the world. Once a week, if we could gather up enough pennies between us, we went to the pictures. Rodgers and Hammerstein's musical *Carousel* was the first film Byron and I saw together, and I was in heaven sitting on the back row of the Majestic Cinema with him. Whenever I think of that film, with its beautiful songs and tragic storyline, I remember the warmth of Byron's arm around my shoulders, and his gentle kiss on my cheek.

One evening, after we'd been going steady for a few months, we bumped into Jean – a nice, smiley girl with freckles and mousey-brown hair, who went to our school. The three of us stood and chatted for a while, and afterwards I teased Byron because it was obvious that Jean liked him. Funnily enough, she went on to marry him, so I was right. But look at me, getting ahead of myself...

My parents, Eleanor May Garbutt and John Maxwell Burns, married young – younger than most, even though people tended to pair up quickly after leaving school in those days. Mam fell pregnant at just sixteen (Dad was only a couple of years older), and that was a major scandal in the 1920s. Couples who found themselves in that predicament had little choice but to marry, no matter how difficult it must have been for them to commit to loving one person until the end of their days when they had barely started courting. They had experienced little of life, and I doubt they could have imagined what marriage or parenthood really meant. Whenever I look at Mam and Dad's sepia-toned wedding photograph I always think they look like a couple of kids dressed up in their parents' clothes, the loose fabric hanging off their skinny frames. They were only children themselves. Despite everything that happened afterwards, I do know that they were in love. But as Mam often tried to explain to us, although they would always care about each other, in the end they just couldn't be together.

My mam would approach every subject in that matter-of-fact sort of way. She was opinionated, headstrong and full of life – admired by those who knew her for her formidable, unflappable nature. I think she was born at the wrong time, because she firmly believed that women could hold their own against men in every way, demonstrating her capability to lead, manage and organise all through our youth. She was resilient to her core, and refused to settle for the life of meek servitude that women were expected to accept in those days. What's more, she had a charisma that drew people to her, and a conversational sparkle that was irresistible. She was so popular that it seemed to me there wasn't a man or woman she didn't know. My earliest memories are a carousel of smiling faces, formed by Mam's many friends and acquaintances, who all wanted to stop and say hello to her and her little ones whenever we were out, on the bus or at the shops.

Even with a complete stranger, Mam would never be short of a few words to say to spark a conversation. Then again, people seemed to be much friendlier in the decades when I was growing up. They valued the simple pleasure of small talk. I suppose chatting together was one of the few forms of entertainment that didn't cost anything. Connecting to others paused the grey monotony of daily labour by allowing people to escape into another life, even if only for a little while. Wise older women would share home remedies for colicky babies if they ran into a struggling young mother, asking only for local news and gossip in return. Men of all ages would find common ground over football, or the latest developments over at the works. Money was scarce and we didn't know a single person who didn't have to work hard and struggle just to survive. But our community was kind and caring, and we always looked out for one another.

Mam was born in May 1909 in Louisa Street, North Ormesby, the eldest of seven children belonging to Ellen Elizabeth Nightingale and William Robert Garbutt. Her dad had died young after being exposed to mustard gas in the trenches during World War One, leaving his widow to bring up all those children on her own. North Ormesby was known, even then, by the unflattering nickname of 'Doggie' – nobody seemed to know why. Like most of Middlesbrough, the area grew in the wake of the discovery of iron ore in the Eston Hills almost two centuries ago, when thousands of people began to flock from all over Britain and Ireland to the new communities springing up on Teesside, holding nothing in their hands but the promise of honest work.

As Mam grew up she learned that she had a talent for dancing, which blossomed into one of the great joys of her life. She was a teenager when she met Dad in a dance hall, and she'd seen little of life outside the three or four streets she called home. Her life had revolved around schoolwork, helping out in the house and going out dancing, and the news of her unplanned pregnancy threw all this out of orbit. Every woman reacts differently when she learns she's going to have a baby, but I never asked her about how she felt when she received the news. I could easily have forgiven her for being terrified – and regretful, because she would never be able to pursue her dreams after that, but maybe she was thrilled at the prospect of becoming a mother. In the end, she probably felt a little of each. She could have been a magnificent dancer – but she also had an adventurous spirit and a passion for breaking the rules, and that ended up changing the course of her life.

My dad was born in February 1907, in South Shields, and was the third of five children. When he was four or five, his father – a Scottish joiner – found work at Smith's Dock, so his family moved from Tyneside and settled in South Bank (then a thriving working-class community in the heart of industrial Teesside). Dad hardly ever went to school – he said he hated it. He would tell us stories about how he had to walk through the school gates with no shoes on, and the other kids would swarm around making fun of him and chanting nasty songs, which is daft when you think about it because their own families were probably nearly as hard up as his.

Despite the fact that he never had a conventional education – or maybe because of it – he was a sharp bloke. He could turn his hand to anything. I have early memories of him sitting in the warmth of the hearth-side with a cobbler's iron last between his knees as he mended our shoes by firelight. He could cook, too, which was an unusual skill for a man to have in those days because they never normally needed to learn when their wives and mothers were always around to do it for them. He could sew with the same nimble delicacy as a woman and he was a talented carpenter, just like his father.

Even though we had no money we had all sorts of toys that he made for us when we were children, including a scooter with wheels taken from a broken pram, and a beautiful doll's house which opened at the front so we could play with little clothes-peg dollies in the various rooms. He carved all the minute pieces of wooden furniture by hand and even fitted tiny torch bulbs to provide our dollies with battery-operated lighting. Over time he painted and decorated the miniature house to look just like our real one, and I'm sure it would have cost a fortune to try to buy such a beautiful piece of craftsmanship.

The doll's house became a labour of love for our dad, but I've often wondered if he poured so many of his wonderful skills into it as a way to avoid the real complexities of family life. Dad was old-fashioned in his thinking, belonging to an era when women were supposed to want nothing more than a life devoted to looking after children. Although he could have cooked, cleaned and darned socks with his eyes closed, as far as he was concerned these were tasks for women, whose place was fundamentally bound to their home.

After they married, Dad was always working, taking extra shifts at all hours and doing whatever he could to bring in more money to support us all. And like most men, he enjoyed going for a pint in his free time. He had a smooth baritone voice that would stop people dead in their tracks when he started to sing, which made him popular down at the pub. People were always asking him for a song, and his rendition of *Danny Boy* had such soulfulness that he brought tears to the eyes of his captivated audiences – helped, no doubt, by the large quantities of booze they had consumed. Even though he was out of the house a lot, we all knew we were extremely important to him. And he was also particularly devoted to his mother, Eliza (Grandma Burns).

In February 1927, six months after my parents' wedding, their first baby, Millicent May – our Milly – was born. In the months that followed, Mam became ill with what was known as 'milk fever' (the medical name is 'mastitis', an infection of the breast tissue that causes severe pain and swelling). Little more than a girl herself, she struggled to cope with being so unwell. The physical stress on a woman's body after childbirth was something people never talked about so she was completely unprepared, and the medical profession offered little by way of treatment. She had gone from being a vivacious young woman without a care in the world to having a new husband and a newborn baby to look after, and her illness left her in a dreadful state, both physically and mentally.

Mam's mother, Ellen Elizabeth (who we all knew as 'Monna' because some of her children had been unable to say 'Mother' properly) provided the only offer of support Mam ever got. Monna took Milly in, on the understanding that she would look after her until Mam was better. This ended up becoming a cause of friction between them for the rest of their lives, as Monna refused to give Milly back once Mam had recovered. It was a heartbreaking situation because whenever Mam and Dad tried to come and take their daughter home, Monna would threaten to tell the police about them. They were decent people, but to make ends meet they had been keeping the family allowance for Milly, which in Monna's eyes was dishonest. To make matters even more traumatic for Mam, Milly had also started getting upset whenever Mam tried to take her back, as she had become so attached to her grandma.

I was told this story often when I was a child, to explain why it was that my eldest sister lived apart from the rest of us, but it was only when I had children of my own that I fully understood what a knife in the heart it would have been for Mam. Keeping a loving parent away from their child without a good reason must be one of the cruellest acts a person can commit, and I don't doubt that this part of my mam's life ended up shaping her into the fiercely protective mother I always knew.

Contraception was not easily available the way it is now and this simple fact determined the course of virtually everyone's lives, and especially the lives of women. Young married couples didn't have television to keep them entertained and instead they would find that one baby quickly followed another, giving women no time to find out who they were aside from their role as a wife and mother. Husbands and wives only knew a tiny sliver about their other half before they wed, which meant they couldn't make an informed choice about who might be a supportive and loyal life partner. Society also put pressure on people to marry and settle down before they were considered too old to have decent prospects, which meant that girls had little time to reflect on the kinds of qualities they needed to look for – and be wary of – in men, before they made such a serious decision.

Mam was in too deep by the time she recognised the disastrous state of her relationship with Dad. My sister Audrey came along in April 1928 and Alwyn Eleanor, our Ollie, was next – in August 1930. Ollie was a highly-strung child, full of nervous energy. During an air raid one night Mam was screaming blue murder as usual, flying up and down the stairs and in and out of every room as she desperately tried to usher everyone out of the house and into the shelter. As the deafening sirens wailed, Ollie balanced on her tiptoes at the top of the staircase, twirling round and round and singing *The Lady in Red*, a jazzy dance number from the 1930s:

'Oh, the lady in red is as fresh as a daisy when the town is in bed
Dancing and dining and shining originality...'

Mam screamed and screamed for her to come down, but Ollie wouldn't listen, spinning in circles and dancing with her eyes closed, ignoring the chaos that had erupted around her.

'Oh, the lady in red
The fellas are crazy for the lady in red
She's a bit gaudy but lordy, what a pretty personality...'

Mam, beside herself and hoarse from yelling, bounded up the stairs two at a time and lifted Ollie into the air while my sister continued to dance furiously, her skinny legs and arms kicking out in all directions as she tried to shut out the immediate danger they were all in. Eyes screwed up, she started to scream once more:

'The lady in red, the lady in red! *The lady in red!*'

Ollie was later diagnosed with Saint Vitus' dance, a condition that affects the nerves that control movement. For people who suffer from it, any trauma or stress can trigger jerky, uncontrollable movements of the arms, legs and even the face. Poor Ollie was only nine or ten years old at the time of the air raid incident, and must have been scared senseless by the deafening wail of the sirens and the thought of the German bombers that everyone knew would follow. It took her a long time to return to her usual self after that night. I don't know if she ever sang *The Lady in Red* again, but I certainly never heard her sing it in my lifetime.

It's always fascinated me how different my sisters and I are from each other. All daughters of the same strong mother, not all of us have inherited her ability to give the appearance of brushing off trauma like water off a duck's back. Ollie just folded under pressure when she was small, although she did become a little tougher as she grew older. I suppose none of us know how we will react to disaster until it hits our own house.

Mam and Dad had been offered a brand-new council house at 15 Berwick Hills Avenue in the newly-built Brambles Farm estate shortly after Ollie was born. It was a three-bedroomed semi with a little square garden at the front and flowers growing on a lattice around the front door, and a spacious flagstone backyard with plenty of room to play – a complete luxury compared to their old street house, or the rooms they had rented before that.

The family had been settled there for a couple of years when Mam discovered she was pregnant once again. Dad was over the moon when John Maxwell Junior was born in January 1934, a baby boy at long last. But heartbreak followed when the baby contracted pneumonia and died when he was just eleven months old, as sadly many babies did during those hard times. Although they had had their ups and downs before this, Dad blamed Mam for their awful loss and this spelt the beginning of the long, slow death of their marriage.

I've never understood why he seemed to think she was responsible for the baby's death, because she'd successfully raised three previous newborns and hadn't done anything different with baby John than with my sisters. I can't begin to imagine what a terrible Christmas they must have had that year, and for many more to come. Losing a child is so unbearably painful that it's only natural to look for someone or something to blame as a way of dealing with the anger, the grief, the what-ifs and if-onlys. At the same time, Mam must already have had an enormous weight of sorrow on her shoulders, having had Milly taken from her arms – and now she had lost a precious baby boy too.

The assumption that Mam was an unfit mother took root, and it began to poison Dad against her. They split up for a while after this tragedy, not for the first time, but they must have been able to put some of their troubles behind them because they were soon back together again. There was no time to dwell on the past at any rate, because my sister Margaret Rose (Margie) was born in February 1936. Dad made no secret of his disappointment at having yet another girl, and soon afterwards my parents temporarily separated once more.

When I was little and I heard the words 'split up' I imagined the living room wall in one of the rooms we used to let, which had one long, thin crack running from the floor up to the ceiling. At first, the crack was so fine that it was almost invisible but over time it grew wider and wider, with more cracks stemming outwards from it, then pieces of plaster began breaking away from the wall. Mam and Dad were always papering over the cracks in their relationship but it never solved the problems underneath, and eventually the atmosphere between them became so bad that it was unsustainable. It was just as our Mam used to say, they couldn't live with each other but they couldn't live without each other either, and so they started pulling each other apart instead.

By the time war broke out my family were back in the slums of South Bank once again, because of Dad's health. He had been injured at work some years earlier when the scaffolding around a building gave way while two other men were working on some rigging. Dad was somehow able to grab a rope to hold the rigging in place until the men climbed down to safety. But in saving their lives, he injured his chest terribly, and he started coughing up spatters of blood. Health and safety wasn't there to protect workers in those days – I don't think Dad was even seen by a doctor. I'm sure if such a serious accident happened now it would be treated entirely differently, and he would have been hailed as a hero.

As with many men who have seen and experienced traumatic events, he never talked about it but the incident had a profound impact on him. He didn't realise quite how serious his injuries were until he responded to his conscription at the outbreak of the war, when he was shocked to fail his medical examination. The doctors said the strain of holding on to the rope had displaced his heart within his chest.

Instead of joining up he continued in his position at Cargo Fleet Iron Works, but his condition began to worsen. Cycling to and from Brambles Farm became too much for him, so for the sake of his livelihood my family had to move back to South Bank. To my mam, this was like giving up a winning lottery ticket. Brambles Farm was heaven to her. Dad's failing health would come to cause him great emotional pain too – his capacity and independence were brutally snatched away from him, and he was constantly reminded of this throughout the war years as the other men went away to fight and he was left to endure the sideways glances of their wives and girlfriends.

On December 23rd 1940, when Britain had been at war for just over a year, I was born in the front bedroom of 13 Lower Oxford Street in South Bank, the last of my parents' six children. I don't doubt that my arrival was another huge disappointment to Dad. I can't say that he ever actually showed it though and I remember him as a loving father to us children. In return I adored him, although I didn't see much of him when I was little and would feel dejected every time he left for work, knowing he wouldn't come back home from his shift until well after my bedtime.

Sadness and fear built up in layers during those years, for all of us. People lived their lives in terror and dread of the German bombers that could send everyone scurrying to the shelters at any time of the day or night but beneath that, everyday squabbles turned into serious fights as families were often torn apart by perpetual grief and the grinding hardship of living through a war. Our family suffered just as every other family did. The next time they parted company, Mam and Dad's unhappy marriage would never be papered back together again.

2

DANCING UP A STORM

Dad's close relationship with Grandma Burns was the source of much of the strife in our house. He called in to see her every day without fail, usually on his way home from work. Nine times out of ten Grandma Burns would have his tea ready and he felt obliged to eat it – I suppose he didn't want to upset her, but this caused no end of trouble between him and Mam. She would also have a meal ready on the table for him, but by the time he finally reached home he was no longer hungry. Mam had a fiery temper and often ended up throwing the plate – and his dinner – at the wall in frustration. After that, all hell would break loose. If she mentioned Grandma Burns Dad would tell her to shut up and mind her own business. When Mam didn't listen, he would give her a back-hander. Despite being knocked to the ground, she always bounced straight back up and carried on arguing. More times than I can count, Mam ended up with two black eyes after refusing to be cowed. Dad believed that he was the boss and he made all the decisions. As far as he was concerned, Mam should just do as she was told.

Mam always said that Dad had two completely different sets of rules, one for his wife and another for his mother. Everything Grandma Burns said and did was right, whereas nothing Mam did was ever good enough – from handling money, to the way she looked after us children. But despite Dad's criticism, Mam was a wonderful mother, blessed with gifts that made her shine at all the countless tasks women were expected to be able to do. For instance, she was a marvellous baker. She could produce great quantities of treats from a single bag of flour, filling the entire kitchen table with cheese flans, scones, cakes and pies made from whatever fruit was going cheap or free – such as rhubarb, apples or wild berries.

One day Mam was making jam in the kitchen while I sat playing on the lino in the living room, when I heard Grandma Burns come in through the back door. Mam asked her what she was doing there, and Grandma Burns told her curtly that she needed some money for something or other, so she'd come over to borrow Dad's best suit to pawn. The door into the kitchen was ajar, so my sisters and I peered in to see what was happening, knowing there was likely to be fireworks. Mam's face had flushed as red as the berries in the saucepan. Dad would never have allowed *her* to pawn his suit on the numerous occasions when she had been short of money, but here was Grandma Burns in her posh coat and hat, sneering at my mother's ragged dress smeared with jam and children's dirty finger-marks. Their voices grew louder and within minutes a row had erupted, the two women seeming to completely forget that four little children were huddled behind the door watching. I suppose the years of insults and snide remarks and controlling behaviour finally got the better of Mam and she completely lost it, launching a two-pound jar of jam towards Grandma Burns' head and only narrowly missing her. The jar exploded into a million pieces and sprayed sticky purple gel around the room, covering Grandma Burns from head to foot with warm, half-set jam. But Mam wasn't finished yet. Eyes wild with rage, she reached for the counter and snatched a kitchen knife she had been using to chop fruit – and threw it. We all gasped as the knife whistled past Grandma Burns' ear and slammed into the wooden door behind her, quivering with the force of impact, before the terrified old woman ran out of the house screaming.

Another time, Grandma Burns called in and started criticising Mam for one thing and another until, predictably, a row broke out. Once again, Mam lost her rag. This time she took Grandma by the hair, seizing the shiny silver topknot she always wore, and dragged her down the full length of the passageway before throwing her out into the street. Unfortunately, she forgot to leave go of the bun, resulting in a large bald patch on Grandma Burns' scalp. I will never forget seeing Grandma staring up at us from the gutter in sheer horror, her hair straggled around her face, as the neighbours looked on from their doorsteps. Mam opened up her palm and a handful of loose silvery hairs blew down the street in the wind. More hairs were scattered down our passageway – evidence of the unseemly scenes that had taken place just a few minutes earlier in the now-calm house.

When Dad returned home Mam ended up with yet another black eye. While the fight was going on my sisters and I crammed into the tiny space beneath the kitchen table, the four of us feeling safe together under the red-and-white checked tablecloth. I was too young to fully understand what was happening but it must have been traumatic for my sisters, seeing their lovely mam being attacked in that way. It didn't seem to have a lasting impact on them, though – such domestic violence was a frequent, if frightening, feature of everyday life in many homes.

Dad spent most of his free time at his allotment, where he kept pigs and a couple of chickens and grew whatever fruit and vegetables he could to help make ends meet. I was rarely allowed to visit him there when I was little but I do recall seeing the square of land once or twice, a tangled mess of grass and sprouting leaves that smelled strongly of mud and manure. I remember watching Dad's hunched figure walking through the misty winter air as he pulled and dug and planted, and wondering how this small piece of scruffy earth provided us with so many vegetables for our tea. As time went on, Dad spent less and less time at home, and Mam was left alone with all the childcare and housekeeping.

'He can always find time for his mother, mind,' Mam would say bitterly every time she broke a screwdriver trying to fix something around the house, or when she struggled to herd us all onto a bus with a pushchair and shopping bags attached, or when she came in soaked from the rain after running to a neighbour's house to borrow a shovel of coal in the winter.

And then there was the matter of her dancing. Dad had been trying to put a stop to it since the day they were married. He must have been happy to go along with her when they were young, but once he took up the role of head of the household, he decided dancing wasn't a proper activity for his wife any more. As I've said, Mam always believed she had a right to a life beyond housework and looking after children – and to her, life meant dancing. There's no doubt in my mind which she would have chosen if she'd had to decide between her dinner or her entrance to a dance. The pain of losing two children, of Dad's controlling ways, and of fighting with her mother-in-law couldn't break her spirit, and she decided that dancing was worth the split lip that it sometimes led to. She'd arrange for family to babysit and continued to go to dances whenever she could afford to. Dancing brought her joy and relief from a marriage that in the end was one long battle of quarrels and fisticuffs – punctuated by brief truces, the arrival of babies, and the unwelcome appearances of Grandma Burns.

One story shocks me because I loved my dad, and could only see him through the eyes of a loving daughter – even though I witnessed him acting cruelly at times. It's hard to believe he was capable of something so shameful as what I am going to say now, but some men lived their lives under the belief that this was acceptable behaviour. Dad thought it was his right to have his way with Mam whenever he wanted to. Audrey told me that when she was little she often heard him ordering Mam upstairs to the bedroom with him before he left for his night shift. She would usually comply, but one night she didn't want to – and that led to one hell of a row. In those days the doors to most rooms were fitted with locks and keys, probably because they were often rented out to people outside the family. Mam ran away from him, up the stairs to the bedroom, and locked herself in. Dad ran after her and started battering down the door, eventually punching straight through one of the old-fashioned panels, before going in and doing what he had wanted to do, and then tucking his shirt back in and setting off for work. Poor Mam. I don't know how many other women had to endure this kind of abuse, but it makes me feel angry and upset to think of it.

Mam and Dad split up for the last time around 1943, when I was just three years old. This time they finally divorced, which was extremely rare in our community. Even more unusually, Dad won custody of me and my sister Margie, citing Mam as an 'unfit mother' in court.

As I've said, Mam was unusually strong and independent for a woman of her time. She'd had to marry Dad when she was very young and that had dictated the direction of her life, but she saw herself as his equal – which was something he could never accept. Dissatisfied with her marriage, she had met a man called Albert, whose wife was suffering from a serious mental illness. Poor Albert had spent years trying to endure a different form of cruelty to the kind Mam was subjected to. The two of them connected through the emotional scars they both bore. I suppose they found in each other a kindred spirit, and they fell deeply in love.

The war was on and Mam decided to try to grasp some happiness while she still could. Even so, I will never understand how she could have given up her children so easily. We thought we were the light of her life, a source of hope that kept her going through all the bad times. But she caved in quickly and handed us over without a fight. Knowing Dad, he'd have fought her tooth and nail and would never have allowed her to keep us anyway, but Mam had had enough and decided she wanted her freedom. When she saw the opportunity to regain her independence and live her life the way she wanted to, she took it.

With no children to tie her to the house, Mam found a job working on the railway – as many women did during the war. But two disasters robbed Mam of the happiness she craved. The first came when Albert was killed in an explosion down at the works only a short time after they got together. Of all of the many devastating events in Mam's life, this was the first that managed to shatter her resolve. One day, she was walking down the street with the man she loved, the two of them arm-in-arm without a care in the world, and by the next he had vanished without a trace. Mam was a changed woman. She wasn't even a widow, with the support of relatives and neighbours to rely on for comfort in her grief. I think it was being allowed a tiny glimpse of happiness and hope before having it cruelly wrenched away that finally broke her heart. And Mam's situation was about to become even worse.

At work one night during an air raid over South Bank, she was taking a shortcut across the railway tracks as she tried to find cover. In the pitch dark of the blackout, she tripped and her leg was trapped between the rails. I don't know how long she had to lie there in agony until the all-clear was sounded and her colleagues were able to pull her free, but the injuries she suffered that day were life-changing. Her leg was a mangled mess. She no longer had any circulation and the doctors wanted to amputate, as they could see it would be no use to her at all. It was Dad who wouldn't let them, because he knew Mam would never be able to dance again if she only had one leg. It was such a strange decision, when you think of all their years of fighting over her dancing. But as it turned out Mam would never dance again anyway. She was left crippled and had to wear a full leg calliper for the rest of her life. As a result of the shock and trauma of the accident, she developed a condition called nervous asthma that left her constantly fighting for breath, especially when she tried to lie down.

Dad, Audrey, Ollie, Margie and I had moved in with Grandma and Grandad Burns at their imposing house in Station Road, South Bank, after the divorce. Since their own large family had left home, my grandparents had been renting out their empty rooms to lodgers, and over the years they had been able to move on to a series of progressively larger houses. Audrey and Ollie had left school and were working, so they could afford to pay board and lodge, while my eldest sister, Milly, was still living with Monna. But it seems we little ones were considered a liability, and were not welcome. Margie was playing behind the settee with me one day when she overheard Grandma Burns telling Dad how hard it was to care for the two of us. She said she was too old to do it, and suggested putting us into a children's home instead. So for all their criticism of Mam, it's not as though they were able to do a better job than her in the end. Margie was horrified and ran around the settee in tears, begging them not to send us away. Dad told her to shut up.

'Little pigs have big ears,' he said. 'Children should be seen and not heard. I'll decide what will happen and you'll do as you're told.'

Poor Margie was worried sick, not knowing what was going to happen to us. Looking back, I don't understand how they could put that thought into our minds, making us live with the idea that one day we would wake up far away from everything we had ever known. I was only tiny, but I had seen evacuees being herded onto buses – their terrified, pale little faces peering out of the windows as they were taken off into the unknown. I imagined that that was where we would be heading too, clasping our little brown suitcases as though our lives depended on it. I had the same nightmare over and over again where Margie and I were walking down a long, foggy road with hundreds of other evacuees, all of us dressed in grey. In the dream, Margie would always let go of my hand and disappear into the crowds of children. I'd wail and cry for her to come back, searching frantically for her, but all the children looked the same and just stared blankly back at me. The more I looked, the more I lost my way, until I was completely engulfed by the fog. I was terrified that I would no longer have a family, or a home, or even a name. I'd wake up in a cold sweat, screaming my head off until Margie came to comfort me. We never were sent to a children's home in the end. But where we did go was probably even worse.

Dad met Maddie in the Station Hotel. She was a widow and I suppose they both needed adult company because they started seeing each other regularly. We'd only been living with Grandma and Grandad Burns for a short time when Dad moved us all into Maddie's house, next door to the pub, together with her crabby old mother and three young daughters. We were treated completely differently to Maddie's children from the start. We were more like servants and had to eat on our own in the kitchen, where we were given scraps to eat from whatever food they had left over.

Maddie's mother was a tall, skinny woman who resembled a witch and was as evil as she looked. One day she scalded my back with boiling water, leaving an ugly mark that lasted throughout my childhood. Margie, who was old enough by then to know the difference between right and wrong, has always maintained that Maddie's mother did it on purpose to teach me a lesson because I continued to wriggle and fidget after she told me to sit still – as three-year-olds often do. Margie and I shared a little bedroom at the back of the house, with just a single bed. She told me I would nod off quickly, but she would lie awake waiting for the old lady to come stealing into the room to make sure we were asleep. The cruel old woman would poke me with a crochet needle to check – and of course, as I was sleeping soundly, I would jump out of my skin. Poor Margie would be so upset about all this that she regularly cried herself to sleep afterwards.

We were always sent to bed earlier than Maddie's girls, long before Dad came in from work, so we rarely saw him. Before my parents split up, Mam would sometimes read us fairy stories about little girls who were treated badly by their wicked stepmothers and stepsisters, but were saved by a handsome prince. Margie would try her best to retell these stories to make me feel better, after we'd been sent to bed at night hungry, and freezing cold.

'The baddies always get their comeuppance in the end,' she assured me, as she stroked my hair and told me all about the lovely jewels and palaces the poor little girls would have when they eventually grew up to become princesses.

Maddie's front parlour was only used when she and her mother had guests and we were forbidden to go in, although Maddie's daughters came and went as they pleased. They had an old mahogany piano with beautiful engravings on the front, and the three sisters were given lessons – but they were hopeless at playing, and we often heard them banging on the keys and slamming down the lid like spoiled brats. If Margie or I had been caught so much as laying a finger on that piano we would have been for it, but on the odd occasion when we were left alone in the house, we did sneak in and Margie would entertain me with a rendition of *Chopsticks*, played with just two fingers.

One day – I think we'd been living there for about eighteen months or so – Maddie had company, and as usual she brought out her best china cups and saucers into the parlour, so I knew there would be sugar cubes piled up in a fancy glass dish. After going such a long time without the luxury of sweet treats or even proper food, I couldn't resist the temptation. When no-one was looking, I crawled in on my hands and knees and stole the last three lumps, carrying them back upstairs as though they were nuggets of pure gold. I sat on the edge of my bed and popped them into my mouth, one after another, savouring the intense sweetness as the little granules slowly dissolved on my tongue. It was only after they had disappeared that I fully realised what I had done, and a knot of guilt and anxiety began to grow in my stomach, making me feel sick. Before long, I heard a roar from downstairs when the old woman realised the sugar bowl was empty.

'Little thieves!' she screeched. 'Get down here at once!'

I remember her contorted, ugly face as she ranted away, pointing at the sugar bowl. I was the prime suspect and I was weak with fear. But Margie wasn't going to be cowed by her. She'd been my saviour more than once during those days, protecting me against the wickedness of Maddie and her mother, and she stuck up for me without hesitation. She looked the old witch straight in the eye and told her that I couldn't have done it because I was outside playing with her the whole time.

The next thing I knew, Margie was howling in pain as the furious woman grabbed her by the hair and dragged her up the stairs, smashing my sister's head against the wall and screaming at her for having the insolence to answer back. In bed that night Margie asked me tearfully if I had taken the sugar lumps. Riddled with guilt, I admitted that I had. Margie just held onto me as we both cried. The poor little girl had taken a heck of a beating, and it was all because of me. As long ago as it was, I can still vividly picture her swollen, bruised face, with a blackening eye and a badly cut lip.

Margie never blamed me. But she had decided that was the last beating she was going to take.

'We're leaving,' she whispered into my ear.

She told me we were going to see Mam and never coming back to this horrible house ever again.

At six o'clock the following morning, she helped me dress and bundled our few belongings into a pillowcase. She made me promise not to make a sound as we crept down the stairs, and I stood in the hall as still as the coat-stand beside me while she went to look for the front door key. When she returned, we held our breath as she turned the key in the lock and closed the door silently behind us.

Stepping out into the cold dawn that morning was the start of a new life for us as we set off on the two-mile journey to Mam's. I was so excited that I skipped down the road and Margie joined in with me for a little while, until we met a couple of men coming home from their night shift and Margie hissed at me to walk properly. The men shouted over to ask what the two of us were doing out on our own so early, but Margie just held her head up high and carried on walking, gripping my hand tightly. She must have been terrified – I was too young to fully comprehend what was at stake, but at nine years old she knew all too well the fury that would await us if we were caught and sent back to Maddie's.

Margie began to walk more and more briskly as the sun came up, and as other people appeared out of their houses she tugged at me to keep up with her – even though I was going as fast as my little legs could carry me. Soon we were breaking into a run as we reached the familiar streets of North Ormesby. We had heard that Mam was back living with Monna since she'd been unable to work with her disabled leg, and Margie had memorised Monna's address at number 46 Hampden Street. After numerous wrong turns, and just as we were fearing that we would never find our sanctuary, we finally reached the house, and Margie began hammering furiously on the door.

No-one answered at first and Margie's face crumpled. She'd had so much confidence in her plan all this time, but now we had actually arrived she realised that maybe Mam wasn't here after all. Perhaps it wasn't even the right address. She sat on the step and started to sob. But then we heard a scrabbling on the other side of the door, and it flew open. We saw Mam's face appear above us, her mouth agape as she beheld two skinny little urchins sitting on her doorstep – one of them with a black and blue face, the other clutching a dirty pillowcase. It took a few seconds for her to recognise us, but her shock quickly gave way to boiling rage as she saw how badly hurt poor Margie was. We threw ourselves into her arms and she gripped us tightly.

'What have they done to you?' she cried as she pulled us even closer. 'My poor girls! It's all right, you're home now.'

We were safe at last. I felt rotten about stealing those sugar cubes for years, but in the end it was only because of the thrashing they'd cost my sister Margie that we were finally able to be back with our beloved Mam again.

3

MAM, MARGIE AND ME

Monna's house was too small for all four of us, so Mam eventually managed to rent a room where she, Margie and I could live together. Back in those days people would often rent a room from someone who had a spare one, because they couldn't afford to rent a whole house. This arrangement benefited both the family whose house it was and the people who rented the room.

Margie, who'd become a highly capable second mother to me, was the one who did all the running around for us, tidying the place up and making sure I had a wash and something to eat. When I think back, I realise how hard Margie worked, for such a young child. Mam was in bed most of the time and couldn't walk far at all. The accident had left her weak and she often couldn't catch her breath. She would become bad-tempered at times because of the pain in her leg, and Margie tried everything she could think of to make her comfortable. My sister worked diligently to keep the house clean and neat, with hardly any assistance from Mam. I can only remember being a 'little toad' who was not much help to them at all.

Before long we were on the move again, and we went through a succession of rooms in the months and years that followed. My favourite by far was when we stayed in the home of lovely old Mr and Mrs Frost, where I experienced a taste of normal family life for the first time in my short life. The kitchen had a huge, welcoming fireplace with a wide fender, and Mr Frost and I would sit on the seats at each end and toast bread on a long fork. He would read me stories while Mrs Frost busied herself making us mugs of steaming milk with sugar stirred in.

But I was happiest of all when we finally got a house of our own, just before I turned eight. Mam's sister, my Aunty Evelyn, had recently given birth to twins. Because they already had three other children, they became eligible for a council house and moved to Brambles Farm. That meant their old house at 93 Smeaton Street, North Ormesby, was now available to rent, and we were first in the queue. Margie would have a right moan at Mam every Friday when she had to take the three-mile bus journey to hand over the rent at the landlord's large house near Stewart Park, but I had no complaints. I loved our new home, where we were to spend the remainder of my childhood. It was nothing fancy but it was ours, and the best part was that we had Mam all to ourselves.

Downstairs was a large living area with a small section set aside as a kitchen, where we could prepare food and wash. Outside the back was a long, cobbled yard with the toilet and coal house. It had no heating or light in the toilet, just a little stub of candle stuck on the windowsill to see by – and strips of torn newspaper hung on a hook to use afterwards. When the weather was bad, the wind would rattle the tiles and the roof would leak – which was no fun when you were sitting on the loo at night, I can tell you! I often had the job of climbing up to fix it, avoiding the sharp broken glass that was cemented into the top of the wall to stop anyone from coming over.

The shop next door had use of the front bedroom so we only had the back one, which me and Margie shared. From the window you could look out into the backyards of the other houses in the street, each one protected by tall brick walls topped with glass shards that sparkled in the sunlight. Someone gave us two old single beds, but before we could sleep in them Mam taught us how to run a lit candle up and down the dirty old mattresses to kill all the bedbugs that lived inside, and then give them a thorough scrub.

'Beggars can't be choosers,' she told us.

Mam had no money, so we were just grateful for anything that came our way. We found an old wooden beer crate in the street and covered it with a little cloth to make a bedside table. That was all the furniture we had in the bedroom, but we were delighted with ourselves. Mam slept in the parlour, as she couldn't manage the stairs. We only had lino down on the floors, with clippie mats we made from pieces of cloth ripped into strips and then threaded together. But even though we had hardly any furniture it was still important for us to scrub the front step every week, clean the windows, and keep a neat and tidy home.

I loved climbing the yard walls that surrounded the old street houses. Mam would scream at me to come down whenever she spotted me tiptoeing gingerly along, but that didn't stop me from climbing up when she wasn't around. I could skilfully avoid the jagged edges, with my arms held out at shoulder height for balance, and I'd take the applause of an imaginary circus crowd whenever I made it all the way to the end of the road and back without toppling off.

From the top of the walls I liked to peer nosily into our neighbours' windows to see what they were having for their tea. Mam gave us the staples of that time when she could – a boiled egg with bread and butter, home-made casseroles or shepherd's pie – but mostly she would cook delicious soups that would last for days, made out of a handful of bacon bones and some boiled-up root vegetables. She had a huge iron pot that sat on the stove and it magically never ran out of soup, no matter how much we ate. Mam would just keep adding more and more vegetables to the pan throughout the week, stretching out the bones as far as she could. We didn't have 'sell by' dates to stick to, and food was always eaten up. No-one had any money to spare, so I can't remember anything ever being thrown away. Mam's bottomless pot of soup was plain, simple fare, but compared to living off other peoples' leftovers at Maddie's house it was the ultimate comfort food.

Mam would often send me on messages and my favourite was to the baker's, just along Smeaton Street. I would emerge out of the bakery in a deliciously scented cloud of warmth, clutching two paper bags filled with a scrumptious fresh loaf, and half a dozen cream buns – a real treat. I could never resist nibbling the four corners of the bread as I strolled home, and most of the cream from around the sides of the buns had disappeared too by the time I reached our front door, much to Mam's disgust.

'That baker's really cutting back,' she'd complain. 'There's hardly any cream in these at all!'

Smeaton Street was an old-fashioned, tight-knit community where everyone seemed to know everyone else. We may not have had much, but we were all happy to help each other in any way we could. As I grew older I ran messages for our elderly neighbours, and if I was lucky I would earn a penny for going. Otherwise, I'd be given a thick bread 'doorstep' smothered in butter and jam instead – which was great if I was hungry, but if a new film had come out at the pictures that I wanted to see, I wasn't averse to letting them know that I'd have preferred a coin! It only cost a shilling to see a film, but that wasn't easy to come by when you think what you could buy in those days for just a couple of bob, so those pennies were precious!

I loved the pictures and went as often as I could. The town was full of picture houses, including three within walking distance from where we lived. My favourite, the Pavilion (the Pav), on Gibson Street, was built in about 1906 and had been a variety theatre before they installed a screen to transform it into a cinema in the mid-1950s. Later on, it was turned into a bingo hall. The Gem was on Kings Road, between the market square and Smeaton Street, and not far away on the Trunk Road was the Majestic.

I especially loved musicals with glamorous stars such as Fred Astaire and Gene Kelly. I could have spent days watching the same films over and over, absorbed in their glittering, technicolour life far away in America. I didn't have a sweet tooth, as most children do, so once I had my shilling for the pictures and an Oxo cube, I was all set. I would lick the cube until my tongue was cracked and raw – but I loved the taste, and still do.

One time, a friend and I sneaked in to watch a scary film, *The Night of the Hunter,* and we watched in terror as the murderous Robert Mitchum found the two children hiding in the barn. I don't know who screamed the loudest! We both jumped out of our skin and hid under our seats, petrified. We may have been scared witless, but we still didn't want to leave before the end – so we just stayed there trembling on the floor, watching through the gap between the seats in the row in front of us until the lights finally came back on!

Mam's friend Charlie was the doorman at the Gem and one of his duties was to check for stragglers at the end of each performance. I'd sometimes sneak into the toilets and hide until the lights went down and the film reel started rattling, so I could creep back in and watch the next showing. Charlie would come shining his torch along the rows of seats looking for me, and I'd know Mam had arrived and sent him in to find me. No matter how well-hidden I thought I was, Charlie always spotted me and sent me packing. Mam would give me the silent treatment at the start of the short walk home, but by the time we got in she'd be asking me to tell her all about the film. So I'd happily roll back the carpet, and sing and tap-dance my way through the whole story with great gusto – much to her amusement.

'Ee, our Joanie,' she would say. 'If you don't end up on the stage when you grow up...!'

I'd started my first school, Princess Street Infants in South Bank, while we were still living with Dad and Maddie. I can only remember fragments about the few months I spent there, although I do recall the faces of some of the children I made friends with in the playground. When we moved back in with Mam I transferred to Derwent Street School in North Ormesby, where the teacher was extremely kind to me. She sat me next to a little girl called Nicola, and we became firm friends. It was at Derwent Street that I met my best school friend, Anne James, and in September 1950 we moved up together to Lawson Street Secondary Modern in Cargo Fleet (where I met Byron).

Anne and I found ourselves in all sorts of scrapes, but we were naive and innocent in comparison to the youngsters of today. Her parents were kind, warm people and I was always made to feel welcome in their lovely home. When they heard I couldn't go to a friend's birthday party because I didn't have anything suitable to wear, Anne's mam lent me a beautiful party dress of Anne's, knowing we didn't have the money to buy a new one. That was just one example of the many acts of kindness she showed towards me – small things, but to a child with little of her own, they made an enormous difference. Anne and I set off from their house to the birthday party – arms linked, both of us dressed up and with our hair set perfectly. We had a brilliant time dancing with all the other kids and I'll always be grateful for those happy childhood memories.

When I was nine years old I had an accident that was to have a lasting impact on me. I loved our school trips to Middlesbrough Baths in Gilkes Street. It was the only chance most of us had to go swimming because our parents couldn't afford to take us. On this day I was walking around the edge near the deep end when a nasty boy from my class pushed me in. I couldn't swim, and I started to panic and thrash about in the water. I can still feel myself sinking to the bottom of the pool and then bobbing back to the surface, as I waved my arms and shouted desperately for help before disappearing under the water several more times. Most of the other children were laughing and I suppose to them it must have looked comical, but I was terrified and convinced I was drowning. Thankfully, some kind soul eventually pulled me out and I was taken to hospital because my ears were bleeding and I couldn't hear a word anyone was saying to me. I had perforated both eardrums, leaving permanent deafness that was a constant source of irritation for the rest of my life. I had to be careful not to get my ears wet, which is difficult enough for an adult but for a kid is virtually impossible, and I regularly suffered from painful ear infections.

My first hearing aid was an ugly, clumsy-looking device consisting of a small wooden box that I wore on a strap around my neck, with a receiver attached to wires which I then put into my ears. It was heavy and conspicuous and amplified every sound, not just the ones I wanted to hear. I hated the blooming thing because it made me feel different from my friends. It did have its uses, though. Mam loved nothing better than to invite a couple of friends into the kitchen for a nice cuppa and a natter. As I was a nosy kid, I always wanted to stay and listen to the gossip but in those days children were seen and not heard, so I'd be chased outside to play. One day, I hid on a stool in the pantry, placed my hearing aid box up against the louvre door, and began to eavesdrop on the grown-ups' conversation. I could hear every word and was in my element until I became restless and moved my stool, at which point my cover was blown. Mam grabbed me by the scruff of the neck and, standing on her callipered leg – which she couldn't usually do, but temper is a strange thing – she kicked me up the bottom with her good one.

My favourite subject at secondary school was British history, which has always fascinated me – don't ask me why. But that was followed closely by art, in which I remember winning my only school competition. We had to paint a flag, and I chose the Russian one – only because I liked the colours: red, with a gold hammer and sickle. I can vividly remember the teacher announcing that I'd won. I was delighted, until I went up to the front of the class to collect my prize and he made a snide quip about me being an up-and-coming communist!

We didn't have much to do at home for entertainment like we do now – there was no television, and only the radio to listen to. Our old wooden radio was enormous by today's standards. I remember being frightened half to death by the creepy stories we listened to in the evenings with the lights out and just a little candlelight to see by, which made it all the spookier. My favourite was *Appointment with Fear*, introduced by the mysterious Man in Black. Even though it terrified the wits out of us, we were back each week as regular as clockwork to wait with bated breath for the next instalment in the story.

I would play outside for hours with two rubber balls, counting how long I could keep throwing them up against the alley wall and through my legs without dropping them. We were experts at performing handstands against our backyard wall, and then dropping into the crab position. I'd be wearing my school skirt tucked into my navy blue knickers, the legs of which fell down whenever the elastic around the bottom of them snapped (which happened regularly!). We only possessed two pairs each, one to wash against the other.

I was always in trouble, and I must have been exasperating for poor Mam. I never took much notice of her warnings but I rarely got away with anything – she always seemed to find out one way or another. I loved playing with my friends down by the small beck that runs through North Ormesby to the River Tees, and spent hours jumping backwards and forwards over it before inevitably falling in. I always seemed to come home without my socks, or with my wet knicker-legs hanging down below my dress.

Stray dogs were always roaming the streets back then and once I trapped one in our backyard to talk to him, give him a drink, and then delouse him (because the dogs always had fleas). Margie saw me and ran off to tell on me.

'Mam, come and see what our Joanie's up to now,' she yelled.

Mam made me open the back gate and let the dog go, before telling me to strip off and have a full scrub-down wash from a bucket in the yard.

Most weekends I would ride from North Ormesby to South Bank on my little second-hand bike, to visit Dad. Now that I was older, I loved to stop by when he was on his allotment because he always seemed at his happiest there. He would teach me how to dig up vegetables and look after his pigs – mucking out their little sheltered area, and washing them clean with a scrubbing brush. They were strong enough for me to gently sit astride them, feet still firmly on the ground in case they scampered away, and Dad would split his sides laughing at me as I pretended to be a cowboy waving an imaginary lasso in the air. Those pigs were so gentle and loved having their backs scratched as they oinked in appreciation – but you can imagine how bad I smelt when I reached home! Margie wouldn't let me into the house until, once again, I'd stripped off and had a thorough wash in the backyard.

One Saturday morning I was on my way to Dad's when a trolley bus caught the back wheel of my bike and knocked me clean off. I honestly can't remember whose fault it was, but it was probably mine. I jumped straight back onto my feet and brushed myself down, but my back wheel was badly buckled. The bus driver and conductor stopped to check I was all right and offered me a free ride the rest of the way to South Bank, but I tearfully refused because I was so upset about my bike. Instead, I dragged the mangled wreckage all the way home so I could inspect the damage properly. Mam went mad, saying I could have been killed, but I wasn't bothered about that – I was just devastated because I knew we didn't have the money for a new wheel.

Another time, when the roads were covered in snow, the trolley bus I was travelling on started skidding and sliding on the ice just as we reached the humped back bridge before the roundabout leading into South Bank. I was so frightened as the vehicle careered out of control down the hill that I jumped off while it was still moving, landing on the grassy bank at the side of the road. I watched as the trolley bus performed a full 360-degree turn, before the poles finally detached from the overhead lines – sending sparks flying off at all angles in an unplanned firework display.

Despite Mam's everlasting soup supply, we were always hungry – as kids often are – and perpetually on the lookout for food. Once, some friends and I were delighted when we came across a field of mushrooms while we were out exploring. We crammed handfuls of them into our mouths before filling our pockets with a few dozen to bring back home. Mam was horrified when we showed them to her – she recognised that they were inedible toadstools, so we were lucky to get away with only upset tummies!

Ration books were issued to each adult and child, entitling you to your small allowance of butter, eggs and bacon – although you still had to somehow come up with the money to pay for them. I didn't set eyes on a lemon or a banana until I was eleven, when they became available in the shops for the first time since the war. I vividly remember my first taste of a banana, at senior school. I didn't know you had to peel it first, so I just sank my teeth into the bitter skin. The teacher soon showed us what to do and once I'd peeled it I discovered that it was delicious, and wolfed the lot.

I was just twelve years old when Mam burst into our bedroom in the early hours one cold, grey morning and shook me and Margie from our sleep. Her eyes were red from crying and we held our breath as we waited for her to tell us what on earth was wrong. And then she broke the devastating news that Dad had died.

I thought I was dreaming at first. Mam sat on the bed with one of us on either side of her and we all sobbed together for what felt like hours. None of us could believe he had gone. I don't remember much more about that day apart from the sadness and the tears. Even by the time his funeral came around, it didn't feel real. We went to the service and then over to Eston Cemetery for his burial, before going to a pub somewhere in South Bank where we drank cups of tea and nibbled on little sandwiches – although nobody felt like eating. We half expected Dad to burst through the pub doors at any moment, joining the men for a pint before entertaining us all with one of his songs. He was only forty-five when he passed away.

I was devastated to lose Dad, but at least we were happy at home with Mam. That is, until Joe Cassidy arrived on the scene – then everything changed. Mam had been desperate for some companionship, what with being stuck inside so much of the time and having suffered so much heartache and loss in her life. She wouldn't listen to the many friends and neighbours who tried to warn her about Joe. He may not have been a wicked man but he was a wastrel who ended up wreaking havoc in our lives. He needed money to fund his gambling and drinking, and he knew where to find it.

Mam had finally received a few hundred pounds in compensation following her accident at work in 1943. After years of having nothing, at last she had a little money and could afford to buy some decent furniture and treats for us kids. But once Joe got wind of her good fortune he wouldn't leave her alone. He moved into our house, and then his son Bill was demobbed from the army and came to live with us as well – so me and Margie had to sleep downstairs with Mam, while Joe and Bill slept upstairs in our single beds. We had worked so hard to build that little home for ourselves and now we felt as though we were being pushed out of it. Joe's son Bill was a decent man, but Margie and I couldn't understand why either of them had to live with us. Margie told Mam we didn't need anyone else in our lives. She was too young to understand that Mam did need other company besides us children.

By the time Mam realised what Joe was really like, it was too late. They were having a row one day when he took an axe and smashed up all the precious furniture that she had finally been able to buy with her payout. How she broke her heart! It had taken her years of work and struggle to make a home for us and now Joe had destroyed it in a few moments of madness. We were devastated – but we thought at least now Joe would be gone at last. But Mam wouldn't press charges and before we knew it he was back again.

That was the last straw for Margie, and for the second time in her young life she made the difficult decision to leave home. As soon as she finished school, two weeks after her fifteenth birthday, she followed a friend to Lancashire and found a job as a home help for an Irish doctor and his wife and young family in Preston. I was only eleven, and I was crushed. I missed Margie so much. She came home to visit when she could and I remember how lovely she looked, all dressed up like a lady. I think Mam was sorry, but she wouldn't say so. I cried every time Margie went back. She had been the one constant in my life, the person I could always rely on. But I couldn't do anything. I was only a kid, and she had to work – and hard labour it was, too.

She worked six days a week with only Sundays off. As well as looking after the children – taking their little boy back and forth to school, and feeding and changing their baby girl – her other duties included keeping the house spotlessly clean, and doing all their washing and ironing. She also had to prepare all the family's meals – baking cakes, scones and pies just as our Mam had done for us. She even brought the couple breakfast in bed at weekends. She was only allowed to eat their leftovers but one day she sat down for five minutes and cut a piece of the apple pie she'd baked, to have with a cup of tea. When she later served them the pie with a slice missing, the doctor was furious and told her angrily that all the baking must be brought to the table untouched in future.

That summer the family went for a week's holiday in the Lake District, with Margie in tow to look after the children. Sunday was always her day off so she went for a walk on her own, but the doctor came looking for her and demanded that she come back. Margie tried to explain that this was her free time, but he slapped her across the face for her insolence and said he hadn't agreed to her having the day off while they were away. Margie was extremely upset and the incident put her off the family for good.

The following Christmas she asked for a few days' holiday so she could come home to see us. But they refused, saying they would be having company: which meant that they needed her to run around after them – cooking, scrubbing and washing – while they lazed around drinking sherry and eating the mince pies she'd baked for them. She could see it all so clearly – her life stretched out ahead of her like an endless film where the happy, wealthy family were the stars of the show but she was consigned to the shadows, picking over whatever scraps they cared to throw her way. Margie didn't believe in the fairy stories she'd once told me – where a handsome prince would come along and rescue her one day if she just waited patiently enough. So she packed her bags and left. The rotten couple wouldn't even give her a lift to the station and she had to drag her heavy cases all the way through the town.

I was delighted to have Margie home – but the family clearly missed her too because a couple of months later the doctor turned up at our door and asked her to return to work for them. Margie refused point-blank. Tough luck! I don't blame her at all.

By this time, Mam's asthma had become much worse and she could hardly breathe at times. She could only walk with great difficulty and was in constant pain from her leg. Her love life wasn't much better, either. She eventually ended up marrying Joe, but they had regular fallouts and she kicked him out more than once. But like a bad penny he just kept turning up again – and Mam always took him back.

4

MY SISTERS & OUR MEN

Mam was right about all the men in our lives. She had a knack for reading people and weighing them up the minute she met them.

The first of my sisters to marry was our Audrey. She'd left school at the age of fourteen and started a job as a milkwoman, but she never enjoyed it much. She had to wake at four in the morning and walk to a field to collect the horse that pulled the cart. But because the horse was wise to what would happen once he was bridled up, and the hard work that lay ahead, he always ran away. Poor Audrey would be shattered from doing several laps round the field to catch him before she even started delivering the milk – and so she left, and joined the Women's Land Army instead. She was too young, but Dad lied about her age and signed the papers and off she went to work on a farm.

I was still at Derwent Street primary when Audrey came back home and went to live with Grandma and Grandad Burns again. Before long she started courting John, a tall, skinny Irishman who wore thick, black-rimmed glasses. He had been recruited as a child by the IRA and made to deliver messages and guns between members. His family were too afraid of reprisals to refuse, but when the fighting took a turn for the worse they decided to flee Ireland and settle in the North-East.

Audrey and John were married at St Peter's Catholic Church in South Bank in January 1948, when I was seven. Not long after the wedding, a little girl knocked at our door and told Mam their landlady was concerned about Audrey. She'd heard the two of them arguing, and thought John might have hit her. Well, Mam jumped on the bus – the stop was right outside our house on Smeaton Street – and shuffled along as quickly as she could manage (with her walking stick and full leg calliper) to sort him out. When she finally arrived at the house, all was quiet and seemingly peaceful but as soon as John opened the door she smacked him across the head with her walking stick anyway, just in case. As he lay on the floor wondering what on earth had hit him, she leaned over him and swore that if he ever laid another hand on her daughter, she'd kill him. I'm sure John never did hit Audrey again – that's if he ever had in the first place.

About a year after they were married, Audrey gave birth to Mam's first grandchild, my little niece Ann. I was delighted to become an auntie, and I remember how excited I was when I was allowed to hold her for the first time. A couple of years later, they had a baby boy, Terence. When the children were a bit older I loved to babysit, which gave Audrey and John the chance to go out on their own – although Audrey complained that it was usually more trouble than it was worth. You see, I didn't just play with the kids and then put them to bed so everything was calm and quiet when their parents came in. Oh no, not me! I spent hours dressing them up as a little bride and groom – I'd do Ann's hair and makeup and use a piece of net curtain for a veil, then climb up to the top of the wardrobe to reach the dress that was only meant to be worn on special occasions. Terry had to wear his best clothes too, and I would brush out his beautiful auburn hair. It had a natural kink and would go lovely and curly (just the way Audrey didn't like it!).

If they had the ingredients in, I'd cook a pan of chips or some home-made toffee for supper. It's a miracle I didn't set the house on fire, as I was never the most careful of kids! Audrey knew she had to hide any food that was needed for John's bait box the next day, or it would all be eaten by the time they came home. That's when they could manage to open the door. I was forever accidentally locking them out and they sometimes arrived home to find us all asleep on the settee, with Ann and Terry still in their dressing-up clothes.

John was always getting laid off, so Mam tried to help Audrey out in any ways she could. Whenever my sister came to our house she'd go home afterwards loaded up with bread and cakes that Mam had baked, as well as a couple of shovels of coal for the fire. We'd pile the coal under the mattress of her old-fashioned pram, which had first been lined with newspapers to protect the pram body.

My sister Ollie also left school at fourteen, and moved away to work as a chambermaid in a large hotel in Harrogate. But she was still only a kid and found the work too strenuous, so before long she returned home – which was when she started courting Andy . He was the only one of all our men that Mam approved of, and sure enough, he turned out to be a lovely, kind and considerate man who could be relied on to always look after Ollie. Andy made sure my sister had money to spend and was always making us laugh with his daft jokes and funny stories, but his cheerful ways masked the tough childhood he had suffered. He was born out of wedlock – his father was a married man, who owned the printers on South Avenue, South Bank. As a boy, Andy would be sent to stand outside the shop until his dad finally emerged and handed over some maintenance money before shooing him away, hoping that nobody had noticed. They reckon Andy's mam had briefly worked in the shop, and the much older printer had taken advantage of her and got her in the family way. Andy always thought of his maternal grandfather as his dad and he adored his mother, who went on to marry and have further children.

When he was seventeen, Andy was conscripted into the army and he saw active service in Burma from 1944 to 1946. He hated the Japanese soldiers because of their barbaric treatment of his fellow recruits. He couldn't tell stories of his time in Burma without getting upset – but he told them anyway, because he said people should know what had happened. If the Japanese caught a British soldier they would sometimes cut off his private parts and stuff them into his mouth, and then hang him up in a booby-trapped tree. When he was found by his mates they'd be unable to bring him down, and they'd have no choice but to shoot him to put him out of his agony. Japanese soldiers who could speak English would shout out lads' names and if some poor bloke thought it was their own side calling them and made a move, it gave their position away and they'd be shot by a sniper up in a tree. One traumatic event that had a lasting effect on Andy occurred when he was boarding a boat on the Ayeyarwady River with the rest of his squad. The Japanese opened fire on them and Andy was one of the first into the boat, quickly throwing himself down into the hull to take cover. He lay still for what seemed like a lifetime, until he was sure the gunfire had stopped. But when he tried to move, he discovered to his horror that he was the only man left alive and he was buried underneath the lifeless bodies of his friends.

Ollie and Andy married at the Parish Church in Westbourne Grove, North Ormesby, in July 1950. Andy was a hard worker and an excellent provider for his family, just as Mam had predicted. Despite his awful experiences he was always full of fun and would entertain us with tales of the pranks he'd played on his workmates – although these did occasionally backfire. One friend had a habit of taking off his wooden leg and standing it up in the corner of the office where they worked. When he left the room Andy would sometimes hide the leg for a joke, but one day he forgot to tell his mate where he'd hidden it before going off home at the end of his shift. Andy was mortified to be called back to the office, as his poor mate had been hopping around for ages trying to find his leg – and he ended up getting a right rollicking for it!

Ollie had her first baby, Stephen, in 1954, while they were living in Millbank Terrace, South Bank. He was a beautiful, chubby little boy with curly locks of brown hair, and I loved to mind him for them. They had two girls after that, Linda in 1961 and Tracy in 1968. The gap of exactly seven years between their babies meant that in some ways each one was like an only child, and Ollie and Andy had plenty of time to give the three of them the loving early childhood years that they hadn't experienced themselves.

I didn't spend much time with my eldest sister, Milly, when I was growing up, because she lived over at Monna's house – but I loved her just the same. She always managed to keep the house clean and tidy, which wasn't easy with five uncles living at home. When she left school she went to work at the John Collier men's clothes factory in Middlesbrough, eventually becoming a supervisor there. She had inherited our Dad's nimble fingers and eye for detail and was a brilliant seamstress, who could make anything.

I was often sent to Monna's house for messages, or to borrow odds and ends that we needed. I dreaded going because Milly would usually take one look at my fine, flyaway hair and tell me it needed cutting. All our other lasses had lovely thick hair – I don't know where my rats' tails came from! Milly said giving it a trim would make it grow thicker and longer – but it always led to trouble because even though she was an excellent seamstress, she wasn't such a talented hairdresser! I would wriggle around in the chair, resulting in her snipping off too much on this side and not enough on that – so I'd end up with a wonky fringe that would have to be re-cut several more times before she managed to make it level. By the time she'd finished straightening it up, the tips of my fringe would be hovering at least an inch above my eyebrows. One time, she tried to convince me that the style emphasised my eyes and made me look like Audrey Hepburn after her makeover in *Roman Holiday*, but when I saw it I just burst into tears! I refused to leave the house until she lent me a headscarf to cover it up while I ran home. There, I had to present myself to Mam – prompting gales of laughter, as she told me the same thing had happened to her when she was a teenager.

'Bad haircuts are a part of life,' she said. 'Don't be too upset, though – the difference between a bad haircut and a good one is only a couple of weeks!'

Try telling that to a young girl who's too embarrassed to be seen in public! Mam found me a hat, and I wore it religiously for the next month until I looked respectable again.

Milly's boyfriend, John Tubby, was known as Johnny Walker while he was growing up. His parents were from Guisborough and they already had three small children when his mother fell pregnant for a fourth time. Sadly, she died giving birth to him and his twin brother, who also died at birth. I don't know if his mother even knew she was expecting twins, because they didn't have scans back then in the 1920s. This tragedy left John's dad widowed, with three young children and another new baby to take care of. The poor man tried to look after them all himself, but eventually he had to give the children up. John was adopted by a woman called Mrs Walker – probably an informal arrangement rather than through legal channels, which was quite a common practice in those days. He and Milly courted for many years before they became engaged and when they did, Monna was upset because she didn't want to be left all on her own now that her sons had finally moved out. Milly felt so bad about abandoning Monna that they postponed their wedding for as long as they could, before eventually making it to the altar in 1951.

Milly was a real stunner – fair-haired and always smartly dressed, with her hair set perfectly, and she made a truly beautiful bride. People said I looked more like her than any of my other sisters, but I never believed them. When she returned to work in the factory after the wedding with the unusual surname of Tubby, she was approached by a co-worker who explained that she was trying to locate her long-lost youngest brother. That turned out to be John – so marrying Milly led to him getting back in touch with his birth family.

Monna needn't have worried about being left on her own, because Milly and John lived with her in Hampden Street for several years after their wedding and their first baby, our Carol, was born there in 1953. Carol was nearly five when they were given a new council house in Darras Walk on the new Pallister Park estate, and their second baby – our Barry – was born there in 1959.

My sister Margie met her husband-to-be, Arthur, at the St Alphonsus Church dance – many young people met their future partners in dancehalls at that time – and she fell head over heels in love with him. Margie was beautiful, with thick, auburn hair and a figure to die for. Dad always said that she could have gone to London and made a career for herself as a model. Arthur had a habit of jangling his money in his pocket, which according to Mam was a major warning sign. What's more, Mam thought he looked down on her, especially when she swore (and Mam swore a lot). Margie had another admirer, Reese, who lived in a house out our back. He would often pop round – 'just for a chat' – and was always kind, considerate and easy to talk to. He asked Margie to marry him around the same time Arthur did. Mam insisted Reese was a much better choice, but Margie wouldn't listen. She was besotted with Arthur, and they were engaged just before he went off to Hong Kong for his National Service.

Being a hard-working girl and wanting to better herself, Margie managed to save £200 before he returned home. They were married at Corpus Christi Church in Brambles Farm in 1956 and had their reception in the church hall. Margie's savings went down as a deposit on their brand-new house in Normanby, which was only a small village with a few shops at Normanby Top crossroads back then. Cows grazed in the fields outside Margie's kitchen window and if you stood in her back garden and looked across the open fields, you could just about make out in the distance the streets of North Ormesby where we had grown up.

Margie and Arthur hadn't even considered buying their own home at first. Instead, they'd intended to put their names down for a council house – which was what everyone we knew did, because nobody could afford a mortgage. But when they went to Middlesbrough Council offices on Cargo Fleet Lane, the man on the counter just laughed and said they had no chance.

'Come back when you have a couple of kids,' he told them.

So it was just as well that Margie had saved up so hard. The house cost £2,125, which was a huge sum in those days. Mam was worried they wouldn't be able to afford the repayments, but at the same time, she was immensely proud. Margie was the first person in our family to own her own home, and Mam told anyone who would listen about it.

Margie desperately wanted to start a family but was unable to fall pregnant, and she had all sorts of tests to try to find out what the problem was. Some of the procedures were painful and she became quite depressed at times. It was so sad when you consider how brilliantly she had looked after me when I was small, and how she had devoted herself to helping raise another family's children when she was old enough to start work. But they never did find anything wrong with her, and it was strange because the other four of us sisters all managed to have our own babies easily enough. Poor Margie was heartbroken, and eventually I gently suggested that they might consider the adoption route. They ended up doing exactly that, adopting a boy and a girl. Afterwards, Margie was the happiest I'd seen her in years, and she was an adoring mother to those children.

Margie worked tirelessly for the first ten years of her marriage to help with the mortgage payments. She always credits Mam's brother, Uncle Wilf, with explaining to her the benefits of buying and owning her own house. Not only that, but Uncle Wilf also insisted that her name was included on the paperwork, which was rare in those days when only the husband's name was usually recorded.

These were the men in our lives. Of all them, Ollie's Andy was the only one Mam thought much of. And, oh boy, it turned out she was dead right about my future husband too.

5

STITCHED UP

Mam needed me to start bringing a wage home as soon as I left school. I was only fifteen, and I wanted to be a milkwoman. I loved the idea of getting up early and driving around the streets in one of the little electric floats that had replaced the horses since Audrey's days of trundling around on the back of a cart. I was even offered a job, but Mam wouldn't hear of it. Milly and Margie were both working at the Colliers factory, and Mam said I had to go there too. I wouldn't have even considered rebelling against her – her health might have been ailing but she was still her old formidable self, and I respected her deeply. Margie and I walked home for lunch at Mam's every day to save money, as we needed every penny we earned in our pay packets.

My first job was on the 'plonking' machine, tacking the coat linings in place before the next woman sewed them up. But I was forever getting my fingers trapped in the needle, which immediately stopped the whole production line and got me into no end of trouble. The more experienced women could make decent money, as we were paid piece work – which is a basic salary plus extra, depending on how many jobs you could complete – so they were out of pocket every time I messed up. My supervisors weren't too happy with me either, because I was a chatterbox and was always busy talking when I should have been watching what I was doing. I don't know how many times I'd be peering over to see what the girls on the next line were doing, or cracking a joke with one of my neighbours, or daydreaming about whatever musical I'd been to see that month, and would end up with lengths of thread whirring round and round my hands and the women beside me yelling, 'Joanie!'

Many of the practical jokes apprentices encounter today were popular back then too. All the women had to go through the traditional initiation when they first started at the factory. I was young and naive and had had it drummed into me all my life to do as I was told, so I took what they were saying literally until I managed to develop a bit of common sense like them. I was sent to ask a lady for a 'long stand', and she told me, with a perfectly straight face, to go and wait in the corner. I stood there like a lemon for a good fifteen minutes before the penny finally dropped, and the women around me roared with laughter. Then I fell for the 'get me a card of buttonholes' routine – much to the amusement of my workmates, who had all experienced the same rite of passage. They enjoyed a wind-up, but the factory lasses were the salt of the earth and they soon took me to their hearts. We had a great laugh together and some happy times. Life was tough, but we were all in the same boat and we made the best of it.

Byron and I had been courting for a couple of years by this time. After leaving school in 1955, he'd started work at Ayrton Sheet Works in Forty Foot Road, Middlesbrough, before getting another job at the massive Dorman Long steelworks in South Bank. I didn't see as much of him as I would have liked because of his shifts – six till two, two till ten, and ten till six night shifts – which meant we could only meet up after his back shift, or before he started nights. One week, he told me he wouldn't be able to meet me the following Friday for our usual stroll around town and maybe a trip to the pictures, as he had some jobs to do at home. But a few days later I found out from Margie's husband that he'd actually been in one of the pubs all night drinking with his mates instead.

I was furious, imagining that he'd been messing me around all this time just to drop me when it suited him. I'd already seen far too much of men's selfish behaviour towards the women in their lives by that point, and I decided enough was enough. I thought I should learn from my mother's and sisters' mistakes and put my foot down straight away. So the next time Byron came round to the house I told him I didn't want to go out with him any more.

It was the biggest mistake of my life.

He came back several times and pleaded with me to change my mind, but I refused to listen – by this time I had already met Kenny.

I'd been supposed to go to a dance one Friday evening with my best friend, Anne, and the other lasses – but Mam had forgotten to collect my favourite skirt for me from the dry cleaners. I stormed out in a huff, as there was no way I was going to the dance without looking my best. Instead, I ended up going to the Majestic to see a picture on my own, and fate took care of the rest.

Kenny was behind me in the queue and we started chatting. He was there by himself too, and he followed me inside the theatre, then sat down beside me. It wasn't long before I was infatuated with him, emboldened by my quick decision over Byron's daft mistake. Mam, Margie and my other sisters were dead set against our relationship from day one, not least because of the age difference between us. But following in the footsteps of the other women in my family, I decided that I knew better and paid no attention to their warnings.

Kenneth Patrick McGowan was twenty-five, almost ten years my senior, and he also worked at Colliers. He was a material cutter, which was classed as skilled work. (We machinists were supposedly unskilled and so we were paid less, which I thought was quite unfair since our work was just as hard.) Kenny was extremely handsome, with a look of the film star Tyrone Power. He was thin, with a wiry build, not particularly tall – perhaps around five foot seven inches – and he had dark, wavy hair. All the girls fancied him, and I thought I was the bee's knees because I was the one who was going out with him. My head was in the clouds, and my hat was well and truly knocked off.

I made lifelong friends at Colliers, people who would do anything to help you if they could. One of the supervisors there, Irene Smith, had taken a shine to me and she tried hard to tell me that Kenny wasn't the one for me.

'The right man will come along,' she insisted. 'Just be patient. You're still so young and you have everything going for you.'

Mam wasn't happy either. According to her, Kenny was far too old and set in his ways for me. I was full of life and enjoyed going out and having fun, while he was a loner who liked nothing better than a quiet night in.

'He'll be wanting to sit by the fire smoking his pipe before you know it,' she warned me.

But I was only sixteen, and headstrong, and my dad was no longer around to look out for me. Since the age of twelve, I'd had no father figure in my life to offer me any guidance. Mam always said that this was one of the times she most wished Dad was still alive, because he would have sent Kenny packing from the start, and I'm sure she was right. However, being young and foolish, I thought I was very grown up to be going out with an older man.

When Kenny told me about his upbringing, I felt sorry for him. He was the second of seven children but as the younger ones came along he was farmed out to his grandparents, who were too old and tired to be bothered with nurturing a child. On one of the rare occasions when he opened up to me about his early life he said he always felt that his mam and dad didn't love him, as he was the only one of all their children who wasn't brought up at home.

His parents lived in a typical street house on Rock Street, near Middlesbrough town centre. The first time I was taken there to meet them, they were having a little party because it was coming up to Christmas. It was a lovely gathering, with everyone seeming merry and pleasant – until I went out to use the toilet, which was in their backyard. It was a dark night and as I came back out and closed the toilet door, a figure grabbed hold of my wrists and pinned me to the yard wall. At first I wasn't frightened, thinking that Kenny was messing about, but then I smelled strong booze on the man's breath and realised it was his dad, Patrick, who was trying to kiss me. I was terrified and wondered how I was going to be able to escape, until I heard Kenny's voice and then saw his silhouette appear in the back door frame, illuminated by the kitchen light. He was yelling at his dad to leave me alone, and at the same time rushing over to drag him off me. I don't remember exactly what happened next because I was so shocked and upset – but all hell broke loose and the house erupted into shouting and fighting, before Kenny ushered me out into the street.

He didn't have anything more to do with his family for years after that, although I tried many times to encourage him to patch their relationship up. I was always secretly worried that what had happened was somehow my fault and I wanted to make amends so I could move on from the horrible incident, even though I knew I hadn't done anything to encourage Kenny's father. It was only much later that I learnt he had a reputation as a womaniser. Apparently, he spent most of his time drinking in pubs and clubs and regularly cheated on his wife, who I ended up feeling sorry for.

One of the first warning signs that life with Kenny would never be normal came when I was seventeen, and I took ill with agonising tummy pains. I was rushed into North Ormesby Hospital and within hours the doctors had taken my appendix out. I was there for a full week. Mam couldn't manage the stairs up to my ward on the first floor, but she still came to the hospital at visiting time every day without fail and waited around the entrance until she could collar someone who was coming in. They'd run up to tell me my mother had arrived, and I'd shuffle gingerly out onto the veranda so we could shout up and down to one another.

Even though she didn't have much money, she always brought little presents of sweets or magazines for me. But Kenny didn't show his face once. He used work as an excuse and, like an idiot, I believed him. I should have known something was wrong, especially since Mam was onto it right away.

'You're wearing rose-coloured glasses,' she would say. And she was quite right. But she had another saying that she used when she talked about her bad boyfriend Joe, or the other selfish husbands my sisters ended up being stuck with: 'You can't help who you fall in love with.' Over the years I've discovered that's so true as well. How cruel that at a time in your life when you most need your wits about you, it becomes almost impossible to see what's right in front of your eyes.

Before I knew it, we had been courting for two years and Kenny proposed to me. I was thrilled, and happily accepted. We chose St Alphonsus Roman Catholic Church in North Ormesby and tied the knot on St Valentine's Day, 1959. I had been christened in the Church of England, but had to promise to bring any children up in the Catholic faith. We had a small do at the church hall afterwards for family and friends. My sister Milly kindly bought the ingredients and baked the wedding cake, and most of my family either gave us money, or contributions to the little spread we put on as a wedding breakfast. We didn't receive many other gifts, but I do remember two. The first was a beautiful second-hand tea set that an old friend of Mam's gave me, which she'd wrapped in old newspaper and packed into a carrier bag. The second was a lovely white linen tablecloth that I kept in its wrapper for many years, as a memento. Weddings were a long way from being the fancy affairs they are today. Most people did the same as us, and catered for themselves. We were just happy to be getting married. It all seemed so romantic to me at the time, as I threw my lovely little bouquet of flowers into the air for one of my nieces to catch. But I couldn't have known then what was in store for me.

Everyone we knew started their married lives just as we did, with just a few sticks of second-hand furniture. Ordinary people worked hard to improve their lot and didn't complain, or expect anything for nothing. We didn't even have anywhere to live at first, but Kenny's auntie had a large house in Middlesbrough and she said we could rent a room from her. But that meant I was back living under someone else's roof for the first time since I was a kid, which was difficult when I'd thought married life was all about being grown-up and independent, with no-one to fuss over you and tell you what to do.

Thankfully, after just a couple of months, a flat became available to rent at 16 Kings Road, North Ormesby. It was on the ground floor of an old, breezy, bay-windowed house on the site where the Jovial Monk pub now stands. It wasn't a big place by any stretch of the imagination – just one large, bare room with a sink to wash ourselves in at one end (this doubled as a kitchen area where we could prepare food) and a lounge-cum-bedroom at the other. It was simple, but just as I'd been over the moon with our first home with Mam, I was excited to be living alone with Kenny in a place of our own. When you're young and in love, you'll put up with anything because life is new and exciting. It may not stay that way for long, but by the time you realise what's happening you're in too deep to do anything about it.

After we began our married life together, I started to learn a little more about my new husband. Kenny said he'd helped dig graves for people whose bodies the British soldiers found when the concentration camps were liberated at the end of the war. He also told me he was threatened with court-martial after he managed to lose a goods train. He and some other young soldiers were supposed to be guarding it on a bitterly cold night, but they ended up huddled around a stove in a little cabin to keep warm instead. When they ventured back outside the following morning the train had been spirited away!

I never knew which of Kenny's stories were made up and which were real, because he was a master of manipulating the truth. You might not believe this, but it wasn't until we'd been married for six months that I found out he had been hiding a large amount of money from me. He had £600 saved up in the bank, which was a fortune back then – you could buy two street houses in North Ormesby outright for that! I was shocked and hurt that he hadn't told me. Following Margie's lead, I tried to talk him into buying our own house, but Kenny wouldn't have any of it. He thought I was just a silly girl with a head full of dreams, too young to know anything about buying property, but to me it seemed quite straightforward – why rent if you could buy? I even brought back the details of a couple of lovely houses near our flat – but no, Kenny wouldn't budge. He wanted to keep his money sitting in the bank.

This was my first insight into his true nature – stubborn and uncommunicative. But I loved him and thought he loved me, and I told myself that maybe he would change for the better. Before long, I discovered that the money wasn't the only secret Kenny had been hiding from me. It turned out that he'd also been engaged twice before. The first girl had sent him a Dear John letter when he was away on his National Service. I never found out exactly what happened with the other one. She probably realised her mistake sooner than I did and dodged a bullet. So, I was third time lucky for him – but not so lucky for me, as it turned out. Nobody is perfect, but you tend not to be able to see the full picture of a person's imperfections until you live with them, and even then, it takes time to decide whether their flaws are worth putting up with or not.

The first person to realise there might be something not quite right with Kenny was my eldest sister, Milly. She noticed he was always washing his hands for no apparent reason, and once when she was passing the cemetery on the top deck of the trolley bus she said she saw him sitting alone on a bench, wringing his hands as though he was washing them with imaginary water. Being inexperienced and naive, I wouldn't hear of it. I thought she was just looking to find fault with him, and I told her straight that she must have been mistaken. In reality, this strange behaviour was just the tip of the iceberg, and would soon grow into something far more serious.

Not long after we were married Kenny decided he'd had enough of his job at Colliers and left, despite having no other work to go to. He was unemployed for a while after that, before managing to find a job as a bin man with Eston District Council. That didn't last long though. It was tough, physical work – something Kenny just didn't have the build for. He struggled to lift the heavy metal bins and was always coming home with bruises on his back and shoulders. It came as no surprise when he started complaining that he wanted to leave. After just a few weeks, he was out of work again.

By this time I'd started working as a conductress on the trolleybuses, collecting fares and chatting to the passengers. I loved nothing better than a good natter, so being on the buses was my ideal job! Kenny wasn't happy about it though. He was jealous of the drivers and accused me of being too friendly with them, which wasn't remotely true – I was friendly with everyone. I've always been outgoing and got on well with people, just as my mam was. But Kenny kept insisting that he wanted me to leave. He saw the worst in the cheerful drivers I worked with, even though we only chatted about how their wives and children were getting on, or what the weather was doing. Kenny and I had a series of rows before I eventually gave in and handed in my notice, just to preserve some semblance of peace between us.

As it turned out, it was for the best, because a few weeks later I discovered I was pregnant. Having heard all the horror stories, I was a little apprehensive about the prospect of pregnancy and childbirth, but at the same time I was over the moon at what this meant. My own baby. Our own family. This was everything I had ever wanted.

6

MOTHERHOOD

Mam had moved back to her childhood home in Hampton Street, North Ormesby, after poor Monna passed away in 1957, at the age of sixty-eight. But her health continued to deteriorate, and the injuries she sustained in her accident during the war were causing her more and more problems. Her leg was now heavy and cold, a block of useless ice that she had to drag with her everywhere she went, and she was in permanent pain from it. Margie managed to buy her a chaise longue on the never-never from a local furniture shop so she could sleep propped up, because she was also struggling increasingly with her breathing. By late 1960 Mam's condition was going downhill fast. She was always in and out of hospital with different ailments, and was now a frail shadow of the imposing figure she'd once cut.

One miserable November night we had to call the doctor out because Mam was bleeding badly from her nose and we just couldn't make it stop, no matter what we did. He managed to stem the flow, but said that she had already lost too much blood. We were all dreadfully afraid of losing her. She fought hard against going back into hospital but eventually she had to concede defeat in the battle against her own failing body. She was only fifty-two, but looked twenty years older, the lines on her face cut deep by constant stress and worry. In hospital, she grew weaker and weaker, and on the morning of November 22nd we lost her.

I was devastated. I was five months pregnant, and terrified about having my first baby. I desperately needed Mam to be there at my side. I truly feared I wouldn't be able to go through it alone, and thought I'd never be able to cope without her.

The time between Mam dying and my due date passed by in a blur of grief and anxiety. But it's amazing how we manage to keep going, no matter how stricken we are. On the evening of Tuesday March 17th, 1961, I went into labour and was taken to Carter Bequest Hospital in Middlesbrough. Julie was born at seven o'clock the following morning, just four months after my mam died. I longed for Mam so much it broke my heart, knowing how she would have loved and cherished my baby.

When Kenny first told me curtly that he hated hospitals and wouldn't be visiting after I gave birth, I thought he was joking. I had seen men and women behave in some pretty stupid, hurtful ways, but I'd never heard of a new father refusing to go and see his own newborn baby. I thought he surely wouldn't be able to wait to meet his first-born, and that his grumbling was just him being awkward, as usual. But I soon found out that he could wait, and wait he did.

Nobody visited me for the first two days after Julie was born. All the other new mams had a steady stream of well-wishers coming and going, but I lay there hiding behind a magazine, pretending to read but secretly crying my eyes out, feeling abandoned and alone. Fortunately for me, Milly bumped into Kenny in the street on the third day, and asked how me and the baby were doing. Kenny was forced to admit that he hadn't been to visit, and told her he'd written a letter instead. Milly couldn't believe what she was hearing and she played war with him, although it didn't have any effect because he still didn't turn up. Later that day, Milly and Margie were my first visitors.

Kenny might not have wanted to come to the hospital to see her, but there was no denying that Julie was his baby – with the same shock of dark, wavy hair and beautiful features. Milly took one look at her, lying there in the little hospital cot, and gasped.

'Oh my God, she couldn't look more like him if he'd given birth to her himself!' she said.

The ward sister pulled Milly up on her way out, and asked why nobody had been to visit me until then. Milly tried to explain the situation with Kenny but the sister looked dubious, and she tutted and shook her head. Even now, people find it difficult to believe that Kenny never visited when I was in hospital having any of our babies, but it's true. I suppose the staff must have thought that he was a drunk or a waster who didn't want anything to do with his children, but the truth is that he did love them, once they were home.

After a few days, Julie and I were allowed to leave the hospital. Throughout the journey home to our little flat I struggled to hold back my tears – I'd had to bottle everything up while I was on the ward, and I felt so ashamed that I had no husband with me to proudly accompany us and offer us his protection. When we arrived at the flat, Kenny was standing in the front doorway waiting to greet his baby for the first time. I was so upset that I didn't even want to look at him, but he made a great fuss over Julie and soon talked me round. Before long, the joy of having my wonderful baby girl at my side healed the pain in my heart, and I forgave him.

Julie was perfect, with her dark hair and skin, and beautiful almond-shaped, hazel-coloured eyes. Her presence in my life made everything better – even though I missed Mam, I seemed to be able to continue with my life because of my daughter. But as well as having a tiny baby to look after, I had a husband who was out of work once again and who didn't seem to know the first thing about cooking, cleaning or any of the mountain of jobs that needed doing every day. What should have been a special time for me passed by in the blink of an eye. Then, when Julie was nine months old and money had become tighter than ever, I had little choice but to return to Colliers. Milly encouraged me to go back and offered to help out by minding Julie along with her own two, Julie's cousins, Carol and Barry.

I hated leaving my baby. Every morning I'd enjoy a few precious moments making her laugh and telling her how much I loved her, as I wheeled the pram up to Milly's house in Brambles Farm, and then I'd have to continue my walk to work without her. I'd go back to see her at lunchtime, practically running down the road and staying for as long as I could because I couldn't bear to part with her, and most days I'd have to sprint to make it back to the factory in time before I had my wages docked. It was well after six o'clock by the time I could collect Julie to take her home again. No wonder my figure soon returned to how it had looked before I'd fallen pregnant, what with walking and running miles every day, and always dashing one way or the other. Kenny helped occasionally, but I didn't trust him to look after the baby on his own unless I had to. Julie was just forming her first words and I was heartbroken when she started calling Milly 'Mam.' It was only natural, because she spent so much time at Milly's house with her cousins, but I was devastated.

Kenny and I were rowing incessantly by this time. I tried my best to make him see that he needed to support his family by going out and getting a job, but it took me leaving him and going to stay with Milly for a while, before he finally came to his senses. This was the beginning of a lifelong struggle to make Kenny realise that he had responsibilities as a husband and father, and he had to shoulder those responsibilities if he wanted us to survive as a family. He'd been left to God and providence while he was growing up and had never been taught to share or consider the needs of others, and as a result he was thoughtless and introverted. It wasn't that he didn't love me – I genuinely believe that he did, in his own way – but his self-centredness knew no bounds.

It was unusual for Kenny to reveal anything about his life before he met me, but I had learnt some details about the lonely, harsh and unloving world he'd grown up in. He was christened Patrick Kenneth but from a young age had chosen to swap his names around, becoming known by everyone around him as Kenny. But the nuns who ran St Patrick's School insisted that he had been christened Patrick, and so that was what he must be called. The other kids laughed at him because he struggled to read and write, which wasn't surprising because he was hardly ever there – he was always nicking off lessons. When the teachers tried to stop him escaping by moving him to a first-floor classroom, he just climbed out of the window, shimmied down the drainpipe, and ran like the clappers down the road, with the nuns chasing after him. That must have been quite a sight – I can just picture them in hot pursuit, with their habits and veils flying behind them!

Kenny showed a rebellious streak at home, too. His grandparents ran a small grocery shop on Rock Street where his mother sometimes worked (even though she had her other six children to look after). When he was sure that his grandparents and his mam weren't around, and another girl was looking after the till, Kenny would climb over the wall into the shop's back yard and collect as many empty glass lemonade bottles as he could carry from the stock they had in their shed. Then he'd stroll back round to the front entrance of the shop to claim the deposit money from the assistant. I think he saw it as a way of getting back at his family for abandoning him to live with his grandma and grandad – but he was still stealing from them, at the end of the day.

Kenny's granddad used to send him to place bets with an old man who operated an illegal bookie's from his house a few doors down the road. After a while, Kenny started taking an interest in gambling himself, having seen how much his granddad could win from a two-bob bet. One day, Kenny put a bet of his own on and won five pounds, which was a huge amount for a young boy – the equivalent of a hundred pounds these days. Sadly for Kenny, later that day his granddad bumped into the bookie, who congratulated him on his good fortune. But his granddad's horses had lost, so he put two and two together and worked out that Kenny must have started gambling as well. He gave Kenny a right hiding, and to rub salt in his wounds, he made him hand over his winnings as well. This only made Kenny sneakier, and determined that neither his granddad nor anyone else would touch his money ever again.

Kenny had spotted the bookmaker hiding his takings in a gap behind a loose piece of skirting board in a corner of his house, and the seeds of a plan were sown in his head. Across the road from the house was a dark alleyway, so Kenny went along feeling the bricks to see if he could loosen any of them. Once he managed to dislodge one, he checked how much space was behind it, before putting the brick back again. Then he hid, watching the bookie's house all evening until it was dark, and the old man went off as usual to the pub.

As soon as the coast was clear, Kenny broke a small window that he was skinny enough to climb through, and made a beeline for the stash. He discovered around £50 in notes and coins, which was a small fortune in those days, and he pocketed the lot. Then he ran back to the alley and hid his ill-gotten gains behind the loose brick.

The bookie strongly suspected that Kenny was responsible for the burglary and he called the police straight away. The next day, Kenny was arrested and taken to Middlesbrough Police Station – but no matter what the police said to him, he refused point-blank to answer their questions. They threw him into a small, dark cell to stew for a while, but Kenny still wasn't intimidated and he kept his mouth zipped. Not many ten-year-olds would have held out in that situation back in those days – policemen were tall and imposing, and not averse to giving kids a clout to make sure they gave them the answers they were after. But since the bookie had no evidence (after all, he couldn't bring in his records, or witnesses, when that would mean exposing his illegal business) and the police couldn't come up with any proof, they eventually had to let him go.

Once he'd got away with it, Kenny went and bought himself a brand-new bike and all kinds of sweets and toys that he could never have dreamed of. He was streetwise and knew that questions would be asked if he produced a five-pound note in one of the local shops, so he walked miles into the town centre instead. If he was asked where his money had come from, he would say he'd saved it up from a job that he never actually had, perfecting a gift for bare-faced lying. As he only ever took small amounts from behind the brick, the stolen money lasted him a long time. He never had to face any consequences for what he'd done, and the Kenny I knew remained extraordinarily secretive, stubborn, and unwilling to put his trust in anyone around him.

Julie was only a year old when I discovered I was pregnant again. It seems silly now, but in those days you just had to try to be careful what you did because contraception was not readily available – especially not in a town such as Middlesbrough – and consequently, unplanned babies were commonplace. I was concerned at the thought of having another newborn baby in our tiny flat, so I was delighted when my sister Ollie told me she was moving from her little street house in South Bank and would put in a good word for us with the landlord. Recommendation was always the best way to find rooms or a house to rent – otherwise we could have been in for a long wait, and I didn't need the extra stress while I was pregnant with our second baby, and still trying to look after our first.

I had the new house move all planned out before I even told Kenny I was pregnant, because I knew he wouldn't want to go anywhere. He hated even the slightest change and already at the relatively young age of thirty, he was firmly set in his ways. When I did finally break the news about the baby, I quickly followed it with another piece of information: I told him I'd spoken to our landlord, and he'd said families with more than one child couldn't stay in his flats.

Now I was the one who was lying, and it didn't feel good. Kenny's obstinate and uncommunicative nature was turning me into something I had never been. But fortunately for me and the children, he fell for it.

7

RETURN TO SLAGGY ISLAND

So that's how we came to move back to South Bank, where I'd spent the first part of my childhood. Our new house was a typical two-up, two-down in Millbank Terrace, one of the many small streets criss-crossing the area around St Peter's Church and South Bank market square. It was dark and draughty inside but much roomier than our old flat. A shock awaited me in the kitchen, though. As soon as darkness fell, thousands of black clocks (a type of large, grotesque beetle) would come out to play. The first time I walked in and switched on the light, the lino was completely black with them and looked as though it was moving. At first I thought it was just my eyes, but as I rubbed the sleep from them and took another look, I saw the last of the creepy-crawlies scuttling underneath the oven and inside the cracks in the walls and the floor. The moment the light hit them they scattered off as fast as lightning, and the floor went back to its original lino texture. All of the houses around that area were totally infested with the same beetles – no amount of cleaning or pouring bleach down into the cracks would kill them or keep them away for more than a couple of days. I hated the horrible, ugly creatures but I couldn't afford to leave the light on all night, and we all just had to learn to put up with them.

We made the house as comfortable as we could – we didn't have much in the way of furniture, but it was home. South Bank wasn't the most glamorous place to bring up a family in those days. It was the home of Smith's Dock, where Grandad Burns had worked as a joiner and where thousands of men were employed over the years to build huge ships that were destined for seas both near and far. South Bank also accommodated the massive Dorman Long steelworks and the fabrication sheds where the iron ore mined in the Eston Hills was turned into steel to be sent all across the globe. The air was thick with smog, but that seemed a price worth paying for the backbreaking, filthy work that these industries brought to the area.

Locals gave it the nickname 'Slaggy Island' because of the ring of towering spoil heaps, waste from the iron and steelworks, that cut it off from everywhere else around. But South Bank was a happy, caring place with a warm community spirit, just as North Ormesby had been. People rarely travelled much, and most lived just a few houses away from where they were born and where their families still lived, helping and looking out for each other and sticking together through thick and thin. I enjoyed going to South Bank market every Friday – not just to pick up a bargain, perhaps a cheap piece of material or socks for the kids, but because it was a social event as well. I'd always bump into someone I knew there and would stop for a chin-wag, then I'd walk home afterwards still laughing at some of the stories we'd shared.

One day shortly after we moved to South Bank, it would have been late 1962 I think, I was out pushing Julie in her pram, when I spotted a familiar face – my first boyfriend, Byron. He was as handsome as ever. He told me he had married Jean the year before – so I was right when I said she fancied him at school, all those years back! I was incredibly proud of my beautiful baby, and was glad to be able to boast of my marriage and my new home too. Perhaps there was also just a hint of jealousy when I thought of Byron and Jean together, but it was too late for regrets and I tried not to let any such feelings show. They were living in South Bank too, and our paths crossed a couple of times over the years, but we all had busy lives. Men worked long hours – with overtime on top, if possible – and my days resembled a record on repeat, just as most women's did. From the minute I opened my eyes I'd be busy looking after the children, bathing, clothing, feeding, changing – plus the baking, washing (an all-day event back in the 1960s), scrubbing, ironing, serving – and finally getting the kids ready for bed before collapsing into bed myself, ready to do it all again the next day.

As my due date crept closer, the doctor told me I could have a home birth this time. That suited me just fine, as I knew I would be on my own again if I had the new baby in hospital. When I realised I'd gone into labour, I asked a neighbour to run and tell our Ollie, who lived nearby, to call the midwife and then come round to our house quickly. As it turned out, a home birth wasn't to be. The midwife was impatient and bad-tempered and the labour dragged on for hours, but I just couldn't seem to push the baby out. Poor Ollie was traumatised by the whole process. She went off to the shops to buy something to eat and dawdled back to the house, praying it would all be over and the new baby would have made an appearance by the time she returned.

Instead, she walked in to find me laid on my back on the kitchen table, still screaming in agony and insisting that I just couldn't do it. Maybe the midwife was having a bad day, I'll never know, but she decided it was just fine to lash out at a pregnant woman in the throes of labour and she slapped me on the top of my bare thigh, shouting at me to do as I was told.

Ollie had always been a little jumpy, but she leapt into action at that. She'd had her own children, so she knew how traumatic giving birth could be and how you need to feel supported, and she wasn't prepared to allow someone to treat her sister in that way. She lunged forward to place herself between the midwife and me, and threatened the woman that if she laid another finger on me she would be getting a slap back – in the face. That was the end of that. An ambulance was called and I was taken to West Lane Hospital in Middlesbrough, where I finally gave birth to my beautiful baby son David on June 12th, 1963. I needed stitches and was extremely tender, but we were both allowed home after a couple of days – which was just as well because once again, Kenny didn't come to see us.

David was a tiny, doll-like baby, with gorgeous brown eyes and a mop of fair hair. Kenny and I were both overjoyed to have a son, but I was also apprehensive about the months that lay before us – knowing how much care and attention a baby needed – when I was going to have a harder time of recovery now. What's more, Julie was only eighteen months old and was chatting, running around and getting into all kinds of mischief, which of course her dad left for me to sort out.

Life fell into a settled rhythm for a while, but when Davie was only six months old he picked up a stomach bug and the doctor said he'd have to go into hospital. There, he was diagnosed with gastroenteritis and his condition worsened dramatically. I took the bus every morning to West Lane Hospital just to sit with him. I'd watch his tiny ribcage rise and fall as he slept peacefully, his delicate limbs kicking out every now and then, as if he was fighting an invisible enemy in his dreams. It was one of the few times I was glad Kenny was out of work again, because he could stay at home and look after Julie. At one point, I feared we were going to lose our baby and the doctors prepared me for the worst. But small and frail as he was, Davie was a battler. After a month in hospital he recovered enough to be allowed to come home, much to my relief. He was still pitifully weak and had to have special milk for three months before he eventually picked up and started putting on weight again. But Davie never was a robust child after that.

With money still in short supply, I asked around for work and a friend told me about a vacancy for someone to clean the offices at Smith's Dock. She put in a good word for me and I was given a start almost immediately – as with finding available rooms to rent, it was always easier to be taken on if you knew someone who already worked there. The job only paid a few pounds a week but it was enough to help me make ends meet and was just a short walk from home, which meant I could be close to my babies. I started at five o'clock every morning, so I could leave Kenny and the kids in bed and not have to worry about them too much. They were usually still asleep when I arrived back, just as the rest of the street was starting to stir.

Working at Smith's Dock was a real eye-opener. Despite being married with kids, I was still young and naive to the wider world and the realities of life under the respectable surface of a tough industrial town. I was shocked to discover that some of the married women with young families would go with other men while their husbands were working away, or on night shifts. I couldn't hide my astonishment when a girl would rush into work on an early shift, dishevelled in last night's clothes after spending the night at another man's house – and I remember being told to shut my gaping mouth and stop staring. The other lasses were used to seeing it all, but it was new to me.

I was taken aback the first time I saw a white woman leaving the docks on the arm of a black man. In those days people of colour were rarely seen in the North-East and I, like most of the other people I knew, was clueless as to who they were or where they came from. Other parts of the country had black communities and mixed-race relationships were not uncommon across Britain, as I later learned with the advent of television, but most of the immigrants who came to us at that point were white – Irish, Scottish and Eastern European folks. That meant that unfortunately, a black man arm-in-arm with a local white woman was a scandalous sight for some people, and the couple likely would have faced prejudice as a result.

I heard all kinds of stories about what went on when girls boarded the ships docked at South Bank. One woman went for a night out with her friend and they ended up partying into the early hours on one of the ships. The next morning they asked for money, but the sailors either couldn't or wouldn't pay up. A row ensued and only ended when the women were hoisted into the air and thrown, fully clothed, over the side of the boat. They were lucky not to drown and were only saved when the men working on the docks fished them out. But they had to walk all the way home soaking wet – talk about the 'walk of shame'! I honestly don't know how they ever showed their faces in public again. I knew how it felt to need money to pay the bills and feed the children, but as skint as we often were, I couldn't have done that to make up the extra cash. Maybe I was just lucky. We didn't have much, but we did usually scrape together enough to live on. Maybe those poor girls were desperate. Who am I to judge? I just can't imagine what their husbands would say or do if they found out what they got up to – and I know some of them eventually did.

Not that my life at home with Kenny was perfect, by any means. One time I took the kids on the bus to Normanby to see Margie, and a smartly dressed man climbed on at the stop after ours. Julie announced that her dad was going to buy a hat the same as his – as soon as he found a job. That was bad enough, but then she turned to me and asked: 'Mam, do you still want Dad to cut his throat?' She had heard us arguing while Kenny was shaving and remembered what I'd said to him in the heat of the moment. Oh, the embarrassment! I wanted to disappear into the floor and if the bus had stopped I would have got off immediately, even though we were miles from our destination.

I made loyal, lifelong friends in South Bank. Whenever we could, we'd take it in turns to invite each other round for a drink and have a blooming good laugh together. It didn't take much for me to feel tiddly – one or two vodka and lemons and I couldn't stop giggling. My friend Jeannie once invited four of us round to her house while her husband was on nights. She'd borrowed a Ouija board from her sister and wanted us to try it out. We gathered around her dining table with the board in the centre and placed an upturned glass in the middle of it. At first we were all wary and kept having each other on about what might happen, and none of us wanted to be the first to touch the glass. One of the girls said she'd been warned against dabbling in the unknown, and that it could be an invitation to another world: 'You're opening your front door and allowing anyone to walk in,' she said.

But after some discussion and a few drinks, we decided it would be harmless fun. We placed our little fingers tentatively on top of the glass, and someone started making ghostly noises, making us roar with laughter. Jeannie decided she should be the one to start us off and asked if anyone was there. To our amazement, the glass started moving almost immediately. It juddered across the table at first, forwards and backwards, then round in smooth circles. We sat transfixed as the glass began to move with purpose, spelling out the word 'Y-E-S.' We were feeling slightly uneasy by now but carried on, giggling nervously when Jeannie asked if the spirit had a message for any of us. The glass glided across the board once again, spinning round and round before spelling out my name – J-O-A-N-I-E – and the moment the word was complete, a crucifix fell off the wall and smashed to the floor. At this, we all screamed and ran out into the street in terror. Later, accusations started flying around that someone had pushed the glass, but nobody would admit to it, and that was the end of our night out. We all went grumpily home to our beds, feeling more than a little rattled. I don't think any of us ever tried using a Ouija board again after that - I know I certainly didn't!

Kenny wasn't happy when I arranged a rare night out with Mary Brown, an old friend from my Colliers days – but then again, he seldom was happy. I dressed up and did my hair as best I could, using sugar dissolved in water as a setting agent, like we used to. Mary was blonde, petite and outgoing and we spent the evening laughing, joking and generally letting our hair down. Towards the end of the night we started talking to a couple of blokes and before I knew it Mary had disappeared with one of them. It was only then that I realised the time – and that I'd missed the last bus home. Seeing the horror on my face, the other young man kindly offered me a lift on the back of his motorcycle. The thought of flying through town on a stranger's motorbike terrified me, but slightly less than the prospect of walking home on my own. If I'd realised he fancied himself as the next Mike Hailwood I might have thought twice. My first journey as a pillion passenger was also my last. He leaned into every bend as though we were on Brands Hatch, clearly showing off and determined to give me an experience to remember. I was relieved to be dropped off at South Bank market square in one piece and staggered home as though I'd been riding a horse, hoping and praying that Kenny would be asleep and there would be no questions asked. Unfortunately for me, he was wide awake and waiting when I arrived home, and he looked at my unkempt appearance with alarm.

'What the hell happened to you?' he asked.

I didn't realise how I looked until I glanced at my reflection in the mirror and saw Ken Dodd looking back at me – I'd had no helmet to protect my head or my hair, which was all standing on end.

'I missed the last bus and had to run all the way home,' I lied (I'm afraid to say).

I don't think he believed me.

My lovely children brought me joy every day and our life in South Bank continued happily enough and then, in June 1964, I discovered I was pregnant again. Julie was nearly three by now and David was just eighteen months old. We couldn't afford another child – but the baby would arrive regardless of our money worries, and all we could do was to try and be as ready as we could be.

8

My Little Palace

The white envelope that dropped onto our doormat one sunny day in 1964 brought news that transformed our lives. To my delight, we had become eligible for a brand-new council house on the new estate that was still being built over in Grangetown. Kenny was his usual uncooperative self and didn't want to move, but I knew what he was like by now and was determined to have my way.

At first, I attempted persuasion – I tried to wheedle him round over breakfast, when he was less likely to be in a bad mood.

'Look at the kids playing outside, sweetheart,' I said as I set down his plate. 'They would be so much happier in a bigger place. They deserve some room to grow.'

Kenny just sniffed, picked up his fork, and started eating as though I hadn't said a word. That irritated me, so I tried the silent treatment next, hoping to coax him round without our words exploding into a row.

I gradually learned that I would only persuade Kenny to do anything he didn't want to by making change the easier option for him. So every time I went to South Bank market I brought back a banana box, balanced on my shoulder while I pushed the pram, and I gradually started to pack our belongings up into them. Kenny looked at me in disgust and said he didn't know why I was bothering messing about with boxes because he had no intention of going anywhere. But I paid him no notice, and just kept tucking away a few clothes and bits of kitchen equipment at a time, and by the end of the month almost our entire worldly goods were neatly packed up into six or seven little crates, ready to be taken to Grangetown.

I'd never been to Grangetown in my life and didn't know anyone who lived there. But being offered a brand-new house was like winning the pools for us, and for a long time I still couldn't believe it was ours. I was delighted to be leaving behind the old dark, beetle-filled house. I'd lived in those street houses all my life and had many happy memories of my years in them, but this was a fresh beginning for our growing family.

Ollie's husband Andy – the kind soul that he was – had access to a car through work, and he offered to take everything to the new house for us. We finally completed our move on a sunny autumn day in October 1964. Kenny never officially relented. It was just the case that one day he had all of his home comforts around him and the next, they were several miles down the road – so he reluctantly followed us over there, albeit after a few rows.

Once we'd moved our few belongings into number 9 Deepdale Avenue, I could finally breathe a sigh of relief. From living in a couple of rooms with just a yard out the back, we now had a spacious home with front and back gardens. It was in a short terrace of four houses, with an alleyway between houses two and three to provide rear access. On the ground floor was a large, airy lounge and a kitchen, and upstairs were two double bedrooms, a small box room, a bathroom, and a separate toilet (which turned out to be a blessing, as I'll explain later).

The lounge was twice the size of the living room in our old house and looked even bigger with just our three-piece suite for furniture. That was fine though, because it meant the kids could crawl and run around without us worrying too much about them doing any damage to themselves or anything else. One end of the enormous kitchen housed a pantry with white shelves and a concrete cold shelf for food and milk (it was well into the 1970s before we managed to buy a fridge), and at the other end was a door leading to a deep cupboard under the stairs. Inside were the gas and electricity meters with hungry slots that swallowed the two-bob bits I never had enough of.

Kenny and I took the biggest double bedroom at the front of the house, we gave Julie the little box room, and David had the double back room. Julie was delighted to have a cosy little bedroom of her own, which was just the sort I would have loved when I was her age. We didn't know whether we were having a boy or a girl, but either way, I knew that all this space would be ample for the three of them.

The possessions we had were mainly hand-me-downs from my sisters, who came to my rescue by not only helping us move but also presenting us with lovely bedroom curtains, a kitchen table, and four chairs as moving gifts. We didn't have fitted carpets in the house, just chequered brown lino and a clippy mat on the floor in the centre of the lounge that someone had made for us. But everything was clean and fresh. And it was my little palace.

I couldn't have been happier in our sparkling new home. It was so much easier to complete my long list of daily jobs when we had room to breathe, and we didn't have to worry about unwelcome creepy-crawlies or damp walls or draughty cracks in the window frames. I naively thought that life would be rosy from now on.

I had hours of fun playing make-believe with Julie – David was too little to understand so he would sit watching us instead, making loud, gurgling belly laughs while we played together. One day the living room would be a grand hall in a fairy kingdom, and I'd whirl Princess Julie round and round with Prince David on my hip (even though my bump was getting so big by now that I had to be careful not to lose my balance!). The next, we'd be in a wild jungle filled with animals – and I'd tell Julie to hoot like a monkey and squawk like a parrot from behind the sofa, while I pretended to be an intrepid explorer. I taught her all the old song-and-dance numbers I used to perform for my mam in the days when we'd roll back the carpet to make a dance floor – going from ballerina pirouettes, to a tap routine, and then waltzing around the room hand in hand. Kenny had a habit of coming in and spoiling our fun, grumbling that I was barking mad and I'd make the kids as crazy as I was, but a few times he was in a sufficiently cheerful mood to smile and clap along as his daughter did a little dance recital for him.

We never had enough money to buy the essentials in our house, never mind luxuries, but I felt as rich as could be with my sweet, clever children. We only just managed to keep our heads above water, but I don't think the kids ever cared because they always went to bed with full bellies, clean clothes and warm cuddles from their mam. I knew only too well that those are the most important gifts that you can give your children.

We were quite settled in Grangetown by January 1965, when Christopher was born at Overdene Hospital, Saltburn. With three little ones all under the age of five, I certainly had my work cut out! Unlike Davie, Chris was chubby, round and cuddly and he was by far the easiest of my babies to look after. As long as he was clean and fed, Chris was happy and content. Within no time he was sleeping right through the night and I hardly knew I had him, as they say. He loved his food and by the time he was a year old he was as tall as Davie, even though Davie was eighteen months older. I often dressed them in the same clothes and people would ask me if they were twins.

There was very little traffic on the roads near us. Hardly anyone had a car and most people used the trolley bus to get around. The closest bus stop was just a short walk away at the Bull Ring on Birchington Avenue, but buses were a luxury we couldn't afford once we had the children, so I walked everywhere – usually pushing a pram, with a couple of toddlers trailing behind me. On the rare occasions when we did go somewhere on the bus the kids would be excited and want to go upstairs but I would never let them, as I couldn't help them all and was frightened the bus would lurch and they'd fall.

Washday was a full day of scrubbing, rinsing and wringing out all our clothes by hand. Sometimes I pushed Chris in the pram to Margie's house two miles away in Normanby to use her twin tub while she was at work. Julie and Davie would walk alongside until Davie's legs started to ache, then he would hitch a ride on the back frame of the pram. I'd do Margie's washing and then hang it out to dry, before beginning on my own. I'd also clean the house before setting off on the forty-five-minute walk home, with the kids and the bags of wet clothes packed into the pram. As well as letting me use her washing machine and hot water, Margie insisted on giving me a couple of bob to help me out, and she'd buy pants or socks for the kids when I needed them, too. I couldn't have managed without her.

We didn't have central heating in our house, so we had to use an immersion heater or the open coal fire to heat the water for a bath. The fire was cosy and homely, especially in the winter. Lighting it was the first chore every morning. It was an art that took me years to master, with many a mishap until I finally learned the knack. First the ashes had to be cleaned out, before the grate was lined with paper firelighters made from old sheets of newspaper rolled up tightly into balls. Next, a layer of cinders had to be put down, and then on top of that, a thin layer of coal. I used the coal shovel held up in front of the fire with a sheet of newspaper laid across it to draw the flames and start it burning. How I didn't set the house on fire, I'll never know! I often ended up having to catch a burning sheet of paper as it floated up towards the ceiling, with the kids shouting and jumping while I beat the flames out with anything I could lay my hands on. Once the fire was lit, they would jostle each other for the best spot to try to keep warm.

Coal was a major expense. The coalman would carry it from his lorry to your house in a heavy hessian bag on his back. The poor men were covered in coal dust, their hands and faces black. It was difficult to make the coal last all week in the winter months and I would remind the kids to take their coats upstairs so they could lay them on top of their beds as an extra blanket if they woke up cold during the night. We often found a layer of frost on the inside of the window frames in the morning, and when I went to wake the kids I would see tiny clouds of white puffing from their beds as their breath hit the chilly air.

The rag-and-bone man was a regular visitor, coming round on his horse and cart looking for old clothes, scrap metal and any broken items people wanted rid of. When the kids heard him calling from a few streets away, they would run in, asking if we had any old clothes to give him. I would try to sort out a few shirts and jumpers they had outgrown and in return he would hand them a balloon or, if they were lucky, a toy bow and arrow.

The highlight of many a week was the gas or electricity man turning up to empty the meters. We would watch him counting out the two-shilling coins, then he'd keep enough to pay for what we'd used and I was usually given a few bob back as a rebate. That would pay for a special tea for us all to enjoy, with biscuits or cake for afters.

I loved being a mother, even though the work was as hard as any other physical job. I walked in my own mam's footsteps, adopting her tall, proud posture as I managed our household. Everything we ate was home-made, just like the food she used to cook for us – stews made from a chicken carcass, bacon bones or braising steak with plenty of root vegetables, or corned beef hash, mince and dumplings with mashed potatoes and vegetables, and I'd do pie and peas, and a roast on the weekends. The kids became fast eaters, as they knew that whoever cleaned their plate first had first dibs on any leftovers. I cooked one meal for all of them, and it was a case of 'like it or lump it' – and if you didn't eat the food put down before you, someone else would. So the three of them ate the lot, vegetables included, or they went hungry. I baked once a week, making trays of fairy cakes decorated with white icing sugar and sprinkles. The kids would descend like a little swarm of locusts, so I always had to hide a few on a high shelf that they couldn't reach, so they'd last more than a day!

We never locked our doors when we went out. Everyone knew everyone else and no-one had much worth stealing anyway. By the time the kids were old enough to walk home from school on their own, they would walk straight in and if I wasn't there they immediately knew I would be in a neighbour's house. Nobody worried about children walking around with their friends without adult supervision. I'm not saying there weren't any bad people about, but it was extremely rare to hear of a child coming to any harm – and we had so many trusted friends and neighbours that we knew there would be protective eyes on them wherever they went. Even so, I wanted to keep them close enough to be able to hear them playing and know they were safe, so I insisted they stayed in the alley between our houses, or on the wide section of pavement just outside our front door – which was fine by them, because they could play and mix there with the other kids in the street. Traffic wasn't a worry, as only one of the sixteen families in Deepdale Avenue had a car. The only other person we knew who had one was Margie's husband, Arthur – I vividly recall how the red plastic seats of his grey Austin became so hot in the summer that you'd stick to them!

You never used to see a dog being walked on a lead in Grangetown. They were always roaming the streets on their own, and more than once the kids came running in to tell me that two dogs were stuck together! On the corner of our little avenue and Buttermere Road there lived a vicious Alsatian that was usually kept securely locked in the garden by its owners. One day someone left the gate open and it managed to escape. It came running towards us with its teeth bared, barking ferociously. My only concern was for Davie and Chris, who were with me, so I gathered them up behind me and stood my ground, shouting at the dog to back off and trying not to betray just how terrified I was. But instead of retreating, it jumped up on its hind legs and bit hard into my shoulder. Fortunately, the owner heard the commotion and came running out to drag it off before I was seriously injured. I was wearing my smart clothes and was relieved that they weren't torn, but I had deep teeth marks and an ugly purple bruise on my shoulder. The lads were shaking and as white as sheets, but they were unharmed, and that was all that mattered to me. I would gladly have laid down my life to protect my children, without a moment's hesitation.

The kids were always a delight to me, and they helped take my mind off the strains of life with Kenny. Looking after them was hard work but joyful, and we never had a dull moment in our house. Once Julie and Davie were old enough, we would play board games together in the evening for hours. We overruled Kenny's grumpy protests about using the living room for playing in, and every Sunday we'd push the settee into the centre of the lounge to create a makeshift stage. I might have been a mam first and foremost but I still loved singing and dancing, and after going up and doing my turn I would cajole the kids into getting up and showing off their talents too. To be honest, I think I enjoyed it even more than they did.

We were all excited when we could finally afford to rent a television. Hardly anyone bought a TV outright because they were so expensive. It was an enormous Rediffusion set with a small screen and only three black and white channels to choose from. Just as the gas and electric were, the TV was also fitted with a coin box, and there were many nights when we didn't have the money to switch it on.

The sun seemed to shine all summer, and the kids spent the long days outside playing with their friends. Sometimes me and the other mams would pack a picnic of jam sarnies, diluted orange squash and a bag of broken biscuits, and take the kids to Redcar beach. We all loved it, even if our sandwiches ended up tasting a bit gritty from the sand! The kids played all day, digging holes and building sandcastles. Once, I took my eyes off the boys for a few minutes and when I looked again, they'd dug so deep they'd disappeared out of sight. I let out a scream, terrified that the sides of the hole would cave in and bury them, but fortunately I was able to haul them out, using a towel as a rope. It brought back memories of the worst scare of my life, when Julie had wandered off on her own as a toddler and we couldn't find her for several terrifying minutes. I was in a state of panic, and the other parents on the beach immediately started a search for her – but I soon found her playing in a rock pool a hundred feet away, totally oblivious to what was going on. No-one wore suntan lotion – I don't think you could even buy it – so the children would come home bright pink, resembling three little rashers of bacon. I would bathe them carefully with cool water until their skin eventually peeled off like dead leaves, leaving behind a beautiful golden brown.

The annual British Legion trip to the seaside was one of the highlights of the year for many families in Grangetown. Most of my friends went with their kids, who were all given a packed lunch, money for sweets, and free tickets for the funfair. But as we passed the club with all the double-decker buses lined up outside, I had to look at my children's wistful little faces and tell them they couldn't go, as their dad wasn't a member. I hated seeing the disappointment in their eyes as they watched all the other kids excitedly boarding the buses.

I used to go to the Legion with my friends on the odd Thursday evening if I had the money for a game of bingo, mainly for the company. But try as I might, I just couldn't persuade Kenny to join so our kids could go on the trips.

'No. I'm not going in there – they're all wasters and boozers,' he'd say.

I was ashamed to have landed my sweet kids with such a dour and selfish father, but there was precious little I could do about it.

Kenny did enjoy an occasional pint elsewhere, and would sometimes walk one of the kids to the Beacon in Eston, where you could buy draught beer from a kiosk at the front of the pub to take home. He would treat himself to a couple of drinks and make the kids a weak shandy or share a packet of crisps with them. But for some reason, he took an absolute dislike to the Legion. I tried to explain that he didn't actually have to drink in the club, he just needed to pay the small joining fee and our kids would be eligible for the trips, but every time I brought the subject up it simply caused another argument. He refused to budge.

When a top band or a well-known comedian was on, I'd beg him to take me there for a night out together, but he'd rebuff me without even considering the prospect. I only managed to get through to him once, when he finally agreed to go to the club with two other couples we knew. As we took our seats, I watched his expression carefully. I was worried that he would struggle to cope with being out in company for the first time in years, and felt so tense that my jaw ached from being clenched in a strained smile. I hoped no-one would notice how anxious I was, but I soon relaxed once I realised he was doing just fine, smiling and greeting the other couples, then later tapping along to the music with his feet. When it was time to leave, I thought we'd both thoroughly enjoyed ourselves and I felt flushed with relief and excitement as we stepped out into the cool air. Maybe this would be a turning point for us. I chatted eagerly all the way back, but he became quieter and quieter until we finally reached the privacy of our home. Then he turned on me angrily, and pushed me as I opened the front door. He said I had shown him up and made a spectacle of myself – just because I had got up to dance with some of my friends. Who did I think I was impressing? He ranted on and on. So that was that, I never bothered asking him again.

Fortunately, my friend Sandra's husband Tom was on the club committee. Sandra told him about Kenny's attitude towards the Legion, so he volunteered to put our three kids' names down as his own. God only knows what the other members thought, because he'd already registered his three children! But it was such a kind thing to do, and showed that Kenny's behaviour wasn't simply a product of the times and place he was brought up in. Plenty of other husbands and fathers had learned to be generous and compassionate, even if they were never shown generosity and compassion when they were growing up themselves. The children and I went on the next trip, and enjoyed many more in the years that followed – while Kenny stayed in the house, alone.

Middlesbrough has a reputation elsewhere in the country for being a poor and rather ugly town, enveloped as it often used to be in thick yellow smog (which gave us our nickname 'Smoggies'), with few of the positive features that draw tourists or entrepreneurs or shoppers to other northern towns and cities. True, there have always been high levels of poverty here, but I believe some of those generalisations are unfair and uninformed. Even from the heart of town, you are only ever a few miles away from some of the most stunning countryside and coastline you could wish for. We might have spent much of our lives within the perimeter of Slaggy Island, but from Grangetown we only had to walk around the corner to find ourselves in lush, rolling countryside, with cows grazing in the fields under the protective shadows of Eston Hills.

I've often wondered how our home town would look if these hills hadn't given up their riches of iron, drawing so many workers to Middlesbrough over the past century. Grandma and Grandad Burns would have gone elsewhere after they eloped from Cornwall. Dad's family would probably have stayed up in South Shields. The mouth of the River Tees and the little beaches and coves around it might have become the north's most popular beauty spot, with rich people holidaying under colourful umbrellas, children and nannies in tow. I'm glad that didn't happen. Industry might have conjured piles of slag, blast furnaces, chimneys and other features of our landscape that are deemed unsightly, but they also give us a special, unique beauty. This is a town that we and our parents created out of nothing, and the brutality of its industry only accentuates the hidden natural gems that surround us.

One of our favourite days out was a climb up to Eston Nab, the rocky point that looks down on Eston and Grangetown, and across Tees Dock to the coast at Redcar. The views from up there sum up the beauty I'm talking about – bright yellow fields of rapeseed, purple heather, deep green forests, brown jagged coastline and a panorama of sea and sky that has an ever-shifting range of moods, from soft blue and grey to the deepest shade of steel. Every time we went up, the view was different, like a moving picture, and best of all, it was ours – no admission ticket or expensive holiday package required.

Four of us mams and about a dozen kids would often go up together, and when the weather stayed fine for long enough, we would have great fun playing hide and seek. From the top of the hill we could also see, in the distance, the streets where every one of us had been brought up, and we would point them out to our children.

'Mammy used to work there... Your grandad helped build that building over there, look... That's where your auntie and uncle work, maybe you can see their car..?'

On one occasion time flashed by and before we knew it the sun was coming down, washing everything in a beautiful, intense orange light. We hurriedly packed everything up and began to head home. Chris was only four and grew tired as we made our way down, so I picked him up and gave him a piggyback. I hadn't been walking long when the low sunlight glinting in my eyes caused me to trip as I caught my foot in the thick bracken, and I tumbled head over heels down the path, performing a dramatic somersault and landing squarely on my back. For a few moments I couldn't move at all, but I soon came to my senses and heard a strange noise that could have been a piglet squealing. Poor Chris was trapped underneath me and all the other kids were doubled up laughing at the sight of his little arms and legs sticking out and flailing in the air. Luckily, he wasn't hurt – but it was a while before he asked me for another piggyback after that!

Keeping on top of all the work that needed to be done at home was a full-time job and I never seemed to have a spare minute, but I made sure my kids were always turned out as neat and clean as a new pin. They seemed to outgrow their clothes at an alarming rate, so finding school uniforms that fitted them properly was a continual job. I was permanently surrounded by coloured balls of yarn and often stayed up until the early hours knitting school jumpers for Davie and Chris, and cardigans and twinsets for Julie – going cross-eyed in the dim light as I counted out the knits and purls. Their clothes had no visible repairs, because I was careful to make my stitching as small and neat as possible. We couldn't afford the hairdresser's or barber's, so that was down to me too. Like Milly, I wasn't blessed with the greatest trimming skills, so poor Julie hated me cutting her hair. I knew exactly how she felt, but I'd make a fuss about how grown-up and pretty she looked, and that would placate her until the next time. No-one ever questioned their slightly wonky haircuts, because most other people had to do the same thing. But my children always looked well cared for, and I glowed with pride whenever someone commented on their smart appearance, which they often did.

Because they were always out playing with the other kids, a frequent task was to sit and comb through their fine hair to make sure they were free from nits. Another thing I remember doing on a regular basis was removing their loose milk teeth. I would either flick the tooth out with my finger, or tie one end of a piece of cotton to the tooth and the other end to a door handle, then slam the door. The tooth would shoot out so quickly that it was all over before they knew what was happening. With three young children, I just didn't have time to be running to the dentist every week with one or other of them!

Kenny was unemployed when we moved to Grangetown, but eventually he found a job as an electrician's mate at British Steel. The pay wasn't great, but I was just happy that he was working again. He had never served an apprenticeship and so was classed as unskilled, only able to do manual labour – and he struggled with that at times, as he wasn't a particularly strong man.

He was paid £12 every Thursday and he kept £2 for his beer and tobacco, and gave me the rest. I was expected to make that ten pounds stretch to pay for everything else – the rent, gas and electricity, food, clothes for the kids, and coal to heat the house and water. I tried to tell him I couldn't manage on the money he gave me, but he didn't want to know.

One Tuesday I had nothing left to buy food and there was only half a loaf of bread and a tin of beans in the kitchen cupboard. I asked Kenny to lend me a couple of bob, but he told me in no uncertain terms that I'd had my money and I wasn't getting my hands on any of his. It reminded me of the way he'd concealed his savings from me when we were first married. For whatever reason, he seemed to believe that men were entitled to go through life only ever having to worry about themselves. On the one hand, he wanted to be the boss and the wage earner of the house – and as many men did, he thought his wife should just put up and shut up. But on the other hand, he didn't want any of the responsibilities that came with being head of the household.

It was the last straw. I could have coped with his uncaring, dismissive attitude towards me because I'd survived worse and I could look out for myself, but when his behaviour started to affect our children I knew something had to change. What I still didn't realise was that Kenny was incapable of change. At the end of my tether, and fighting back tears of frustration I made one final attempt to trigger a reaction, threatening him with an ultimatum:

'If that's your attitude maybe I should just take the kids and go – we'd be better off without you anyway!' I screamed at him.

I studied his face for any hint of recognition of the pain I was feeling, for a flicker of remorse or guilt or shame that he had driven me to this point – but he didn't seem troubled in the least.

'It's my name on the rent book, so you're free to take the kids and leave if you want,' he said indifferently. 'I'm not going anywhere.'

So that was that. Thank God my lovely friends and sisters had husbands who were better providers than him, and they were always willing to sub me a few shillings until Kenny's next pay-day, even if he wouldn't. At least he finally had work, I told myself. But as they say, be careful what you wish for. Working in the polluted environment at British Steel was to be the catalyst for Kenny's already odd behaviour to take a disastrous turn for the worse.

9

—·—

SOAP

I don't remember exactly when Kenny's conduct stopped being merely eccentric, and started making life unbearable for everyone else in the family. I suppose it was a gradual process. He'd always been particular about washing his hands regularly and would only wear certain clothes. He would never let me choose anything for him as other wives did, but I let that go. Let him be stubborn and buy his own socks, I thought – it was one less job for me to worry about. But after he started working at British Steel, his behaviour became dramatically worse.

I don't know if he put overalls on top when he arrived at work, but the get-up Kenny always wore when he left for a shift was a pair of ancient Crimplene trousers, a raggedy-necked shirt with a t-shirt underneath, and his donkey jacket. He kept his work clothes in the walk-in kitchen cupboard that led to the nook under the stairs, and apart from when he was wearing them, they were only ever taken out so I could wash them. When it was time for him to leave for work he would go upstairs and take off his everyday clothes and then run back down the stairs completely naked, covering his privates if anyone was around. Because the cupboard was in the kitchen, he had to scurry his way through the whole house without a stitch on him – even in the winter months.

It didn't bother me so much when he was on an early shift starting at six in the morning, and there was only our family in the house. The children were still asleep in bed at that time of the morning, at least. The problem with this strange habit was when he returned home at two-thirty in the afternoon and wanted to go through the same rigmarole in reverse, shedding his clothes in the hallway and dumping them back in the cupboard for me to deal with, before dashing up to the bathroom. The days were long and lonely when the kids were at school and I often invited friends round for a cuppa and a natter, or sometimes they'd drop in unexpectedly. When Kenny arrived home he would want to take his clothes off downstairs immediately, so he could go straight up to his bath. If I had guests, I had to ask them to leave – but I wasn't allowed to tell them why, which was awkward and embarrassing. Whenever he had to wait more than half an hour or so before they left, he would be in a foul mood and wouldn't speak to me. The second the door closed behind them, he would strip off completely naked and dart up to the bathroom without saying a word.

Occasionally, if one of my sisters was around, Kenny would have a cup of tea with us – but soon the thought of the dirt on his body would become too much for him to bear and he would say, 'I need my bath now' – and we'd have to go outside into the back garden for five minutes to give him time to strip off, throw his clothes in the cupboard, and run up to the bathroom.

As far as Kenny was concerned, once that cupboard door was closed, all the filth and contamination was safely locked away. If anyone needed to go in there, there would be hell on. He even banned me from going in to top up the gas and electric meters (if he was in the house) because he was convinced that merely opening the door would let the germs out. I had to make sure I'd put in enough coins before he arrived home from work, because if the lights went out during the evening, we weren't allowed to do anything about it – so we all had to go to bed early, or sit in the dark.

On top of the difficulties this added to our life, I couldn't help but see a deeper meaning to all this. Kenny felt that the dirt was too dangerous to touch any part of *him* – maybe he'd been warned about toxic substances at work, and that must have thoroughly frightened him – but he didn't seem to care if any of it infected me or the kids. Daily, I would find myself elbow-deep in water stained dark brown by the dust and dirt from his clothes, as I scrubbed and lathered and rinsed the fabric between my fingers – the same filth that he couldn't bear to touch or even look at. So concerned was he about the contamination, that he was willing to pass it on to his nearest and dearest.

Eventually he fixed on one set of work clothes and refused to go to work in anything else, so I struggled to wash and dry them in time if he had a quick shift changeover. Instead, I would have to take his dirty clothes outside to beat and shake the grime off them, trying not to inhale the dust that would rise up in a great cloud, before I hung them on the line to at least freshen them up for him.

I also worried about the psychological impact on the kids of having to see their father bizarrely sprinting naked around the house every day. Julie was our only girl, and I became increasingly concerned on her behalf as she approached her teenage years. I told him it just wasn't right and begged him to at least wrap a towel around his waist. Kenny had a strong sense of propriety when it came to women – he hated me dancing or drinking or speaking to other men, because it wasn't appropriate for a wife and mother, but those rules didn't seem to apply to him. He told me I was the one being ridiculous, and that what he did wasn't unusual – and besides, he was the breadwinner, so he could do as he pleased in his own house.

It was ironic that we didn't even have a proper bathroom until we moved to Grangetown, but the clean, modern facilities in the new house seemed to make Kenny's problems worse instead of better. To start with, it only took him half an hour to wash himself thoroughly, and I didn't think much of it. But the length of time he stayed in the bath began to creep up over the months, stretching to an hour and more. I remember breaking down in tears because I couldn't keep up with the bars of Palmolive soap he was going through and he wouldn't give me money for any more, so I had to forgo my own toiletries just to be able to afford soap to wash the kids with.

Thank God we had a separate toilet besides the bathroom, otherwise I don't know what we would have done. One day I popped up to use the loo and heard a strange, rhythmic counting coming from next door. When I peeked in to the bathroom to see what it was, I was greeted by the strangest sight. Kenny was sitting in the bath with just his two eyes peering out and the rest of him covered in soapy lather. He resembled a melting snowman. He continued counting out loud as he methodically scrubbed each limb of his body. I couldn't take in what I was seeing – but that was just the start of it.

At first he'd only count to ten or twenty before moving on to the next arm, leg or foot, but over time I know it reached a tally of a hundred and more. I'd send the kids to tell him to hurry up because his dinner was ready but if he was interrupted it only made matters worse, and he'd end up staying in there even longer because he had to start counting again from scratch.

Once he knew I was aware of this ritual, he decided it would become another of my responsibilities. Convinced germs were lurking invisibly on his body, he started banging on the floor and insisting that I go up to the bathroom and scrub his back whenever he called. I had to go in and follow his instructions to the letter, washing him with the horrible slimy rag of a flannel he used. First I had to work in a line from left to right, and once that was done to his satisfaction I had to start scrubbing in rows from top to bottom, a soapy game of noughts and crosses that nobody ever won.

The irony of it was that the flannel was probably full of germs. It was impossible to keep properly clean because it was used so frequently, and he would only replace it when it was completely frayed and raggy. He was no help keeping the bathroom clean either, so since the whole family was using it I don't suppose it was the most sterile place he could have been. Giving the bath a quick scrub when he was finished and putting down some bleach seemed to be beyond his capabilities. His idea of what it meant for something or someone to be 'contaminated' was something I could never quite pin down, because it didn't appear to apply to certain objects, and he never seemed bothered about the general cleanliness of the house.

If I was too busy and ignored his cries, he refused to come out of the bath at all until the water was icy cold and his teeth were chattering, so I started sending one of the kids up to help him instead. By now, Julie could be quite cheeky towards Kenny, knowing he wouldn't dare touch her because he thought the kids were unclean. One day he told her she'd missed a bit and had to do it all over again, and she decided she'd had enough. I heard a commotion coming from upstairs as she flung the flannel across the bathroom.

'If you're not happy with the way I do it, then do it yourself!' she shouted, and stormed out. Everything went quiet for a few moments and then I heard the familiar sound of Kenny braying through the ceiling.

'JOANIE!' he shouted. 'Come up! I need you to come and wash my back! JOANIEEE!'

And so our family life continued, revolving around Kenny's compulsions and paranoia.

British Steel could be a dangerous environment and we were always hearing about accidents, some of them fatal. It must have been a frightening and depressing place to work at times. Kenny was devastated when the electrician he had worked alongside for years weighed himself down with bricks and jumped into the settling pool at their plant. What a horrible way to die. Kenny was devastated, and I often wondered whether it was this tragedy that made Kenny's illness become so much worse. I knew he wasn't right, and began to worry myself sick about him – but no matter how much I pleaded with him, he always turned it back onto me.

The situation rapidly deteriorated after that. His bath-time routine escalated from an hour to three and four hours, and sometimes even more. As soon as the front door was closed behind him after he came in from work, off came his clothes and that would be it from him until the end of the night.

He'd be scrubbing away at his skin until bedtime, emerging back out of the bathroom in a cloud of steam, patches of red sores all over his body.

Providing enough hot water to keep his bath topped up while he went through his painstaking ritual was backbreaking work. The immersion heater went through money so fast that I quickly ran out of coins for the meter. That meant all year round, even when the sun was burning down in the middle of summer, we would have the fire roaring up the chimney to heat the back boiler. Soon he was staying in the bath for so long that even the coal fire couldn't heat enough water for him. I would have to fill the gas boiler in the kitchen and then carry hot water upstairs to him in buckets to pour into the bath. If I told him to make do with the water he already had, he would start banging on the floor again, shouting that he wasn't coming out of the bath until he was sure he had washed every bit of dirt from his body.

Life was busy enough taking care of almost every responsibility associated with our household and family, and now I became Kenny's water-carrying slave, hoisting gallons of hot water up the stairs hour after hour. When he arrived home after a two-till-ten shift I would find myself standing half-asleep outside the bathroom in the early hours of the morning, begging him to get out of the bath and come to bed as I pressed my sweating forehead against the cool wooden door, my hands red raw and covered in scalds. Every night I found myself too tired to think, but I was petrified that he would catch a cold or worse, pneumonia, if I allowed him to sit in a freezing cold bath. We desperately needed the money he was bringing home, even if he was spending half of it on hot water and soap.

Back then I didn't know Kenny's illness had a name, but I do now – Obsessive Compulsive Disorder, or OCD. Try as I might, I couldn't understand why Kenny behaved the way he did, and I felt powerless to do anything about it. I was desperate to find him some help, but I didn't know what to do or who to speak to about him. He had made it plain over our years of marriage that he had no respect for my opinion, or for anything I might suggest. I couldn't ask for advice from anyone I knew because mental health was not a topic people spoke openly about in those days. There was a great deal of ignorance concerning psychological problems, and stigma was attached to anyone who experienced them.

We were completely unequipped when it came to Kenny, without even the right words to describe his condition. I tried to confide in my sisters – but although they couldn't hide their astonishment at what I told them, I'm sure they thought I was exaggerating. Some people are just particular about hygiene. Maybe they even thought I should be thankful, because they might have been glad if their husbands had been a bit more concerned about cleanliness. Margie eventually said I should make Kenny go to the doctor, but how could I persuade him to go? He didn't even like me taking the kids to the doctor's. The idea of going there himself was something he couldn't contemplate.

When I pointed out to him as gently as I could that his problems were getting worse, he just snarled at me.

'The so-called problems are in your head, not mine. You're the one who's going crazy!'

His insistence that he simply liked to be clean and that there was nothing unusual about his behaviour made me doubt my own sanity at times. But I knew the clock didn't lie, and my aching arms from carrying endless buckets of water up the stairs weren't a figment of my imagination. I kept asking our GP to come to the house to see him and he finally agreed – but unfortunately Kenny spotted his car pulling up outside the house, and before the doctor had a chance to speak to him he'd shot out the back door, leapt over the fence and run off.

As much as Kenny insisted that everything he did was perfectly normal, I believe he had a deep-seated fear of anyone else knowing what he did behind the closed doors of our home. I was safe, because he didn't care what I thought – but when it came to other people, he was deathly afraid that he would be exposed and written off as a madman. In one last attempt to involve the medical profession I went to the surgery and begged for help, but I was told that the doctor couldn't do anything unless Kenny came in himself – and by this time I knew it was hopeless to try to make him go. After all, there was nothing wrong with him, was there? – it was all in my imagination.

10

—.—

FRIENDS AND NEIGHBOURS

Some of my old friends had moved to Grangetown with us, but I also formed friendships with our new neighbours, lovely lasses with young families just like mine. One of the simple pleasures I most enjoyed was the opportunity to chat across the fence with Sheena next door, when Kenny was at work and the house was peaceful at last. Our neighbours on the other side, sharing the alley, were the Simpsons and their four boys, who were all around the same age as our kids. They knocked about together and were great pals – although they occasionally fell out, and it was always up to us adults to encourage them to make amends. One day I glanced out of our front window to see one of their boys holding our Chris's arms while the other one hit him. Without thinking twice, I leapt straight out of the window and ran across the road to drag them apart!

Further along the road lived the Bensons, Sandra and her husband Tom. We'd all moved into Deepdale Avenue at about the same time, and they became great friends of ours – he was the lovely man who gave us tickets for the British Legion trips. Their Denise was just a year older than Julie, and their boys were the same ages as Davie and Chris.

Sandra was a lovely lass but she couldn't bear the sight of blood and was hopeless when her kids hurt themselves. She would look away and shoo them along to my house, where I bandaged their fingers and cleaned up their scuffed knees. I say 'bandaged', although I didn't have any proper dressings or plasters – I couldn't afford them – so I'd run a strip off a clean sheet and use that. As a result we didn't have a sheet in the house that didn't have a frayed edge and the end missing, so none of them quite fitted the mattresses! I didn't mind, though, because we helped each other out in different ways. I looked after Sandra's kids if she had a message she needed to run, and she would return the favour for me. Once, I looked after them for the afternoon and she came along afterwards to ask me what I'd given them for their tea. Her toddler Tony had told her that Joanie had given him little eggs on toast and he wanted some more. I burst out laughing – it must have been Tony's first experience of baked beans!

Tom worked away from home, so Sandra was often left alone with the kids. She enjoyed company and would regularly pop round the corner to the Legion in the evening. During the light summer nights all the local kids played outside in the street until late, but Sandra would bring her three in early and change them into their pyjamas ready for bed so she could head off to the club. But as soon as she was out of sight, the kids would dash straight back outside again to carry on playing with their friends. A problem would only arise if they happened to fall and scuff their knees, or if they went back in at the end of the night and the electricity had run out. Denise would knock on our door, as they were afraid of the dark – and of course I would end up putting my two shillings in their meter because they were by themselves and I couldn't leave them in the pitch black. Me and our kids would then have to have another early night, since I wouldn't have any coins left for our own meter!

Most of the neighbours were the salt of the earth, but there were a few tyrants living around the estate who caused misery to their families. Kenny was a saint compared to some of them. Billy Jones, who lived in one of the houses out our back, was a bully who terrorised his wife and children. It seemed as if they could never do anything right, and he was forever bellowing at them and putting them down. Sometimes he would lock them out of the house, no matter what the weather was doing. His kids used to cower when he came near because they were so frightened of him, and I even saw them using their back garden as a toilet sometimes, because they didn't dare go back into the house.

I wasn't intimidated by him, though. I'd seen enough bullies in my life to know they are all cowards at heart. One day he refused to give our kids their ball back after it went into his garden, even though I heard Julie asking politely if she could go in for it. He swore at her and said he was sick of the noise they were making and would only return it when he was good and ready, and not before. I was incensed, and marched down to the bottom of our garden, shouting at him to come back out. Billy was a menacing presence, well over six feet tall and stockily built (albeit with an overhanging beer belly) and their garden was slightly elevated from ours, making him tower over me even more.

'You need to learn how to control those brats of yours, kicking their ball in here and damaging my flowers,' he ranted.

To his surprise, instead of backing down, I stood my ground and looked him straight in the eye.

'You don't scare me in the slightest,' I told him. 'My children are well behaved and well mannered, unlike you, and they're not bothering anyone.'

When it came to my kids, I had my mother's fiery blood, and I saw red whenever anyone threatened them. Billy wasn't used to being put in his place, especially not by a woman. His neck and face turned bright red and I thought he was going to blow a gasket, but I wasn't finished yet.

'If you don't give them their ball I'm going to climb over that fence and bring it back myself!'

He knew he was beaten and grudgingly handed it over to me, but he continued swearing and making derogatory comments about women as he did so. I just smiled serenely and threw the ball to the kids, with some satisfaction.

'And if I ever hear you swearing at my kids again, I'll be back round here to deal with you,' I called to him as I stepped off his property.

Later that evening Julie told me she was petrified he was going to hit me, and had run inside to tell her dad.

'Your mother's got herself into it, she can get herself out of it,' Kenny told her, and he carried on reading his paper.

He was probably right to stay indoors, as the picture might have turned uglier if he had come to my aid. It was typical of Kenny, though. He never involved himself in anything to do with the children – that was my department. He always referred to them as 'your' kids, as though he'd had nothing to do with them coming into the world!

My friend Eileen's husband was a serious gambler and another ogre. He would send her running to the bookies round the corner on Slater Road to place his bet with only a few minutes to spare before the race started. If she didn't make it in time, poor Eileen would be too afraid to go back home – and their unfortunate kids seemed terrified whenever their dad was around.

The Child Support Agency didn't exist in those days, and only a few of the women I knew whose husbands deserted them were ever paid any maintenance for the children. The social security money they received was nowhere near enough to cover the cost of a family's basic essentials, so friends and neighbours would do whatever they could to help out. Linda, an old friend of mine from our South Bank days, moved to the estate shortly after us, but her husband upped and left her with two young kids to bring up on her own. I was shocked when she told me how his full cousin had come into their lives out of nowhere, and before she knew it the pair had run off together. Linda loved her husband and the poor lass was heartbroken. She had no idea where he had disappeared to, and didn't hear from him throughout all the years the kids were growing up. I felt desperately sorry for her, and did my best to support her in whatever ways I could. And I have to say, she always did the same for me in return.

The husband of another of my close friends, Sue, also left her in the lurch with four young kids to support. I tried to be a good friend and would keep an eye on her little ones and pass on hand-me-downs whenever I could. We women had to look out for one another because we knew nobody else would.

Kenny never bothered much with any of the other men. He spoke to the neighbours but he didn't have any real male friends, and he just seemed to enjoy his own company. I don't even know if he had any mates at work, but if he did he never said a single word about them. Then again, he didn't tell me anything about his job. I don't actually know what it was he did, beyond the start and finish times of his shifts and the fact that his work was classed as unskilled.

Over the years some of our neighbours moved on, and I lost old friends and made some new ones. When Sheena next door moved to Eston, Penny moved in with her four children. She was originally from Cornwall but had married a Middlesbrough man. Penny was another poor lass who was left to bring up her young family alone when the marriage broke down, and she didn't even have friends or relatives to fall back on. Sadly, she was ill-equipped for the thankless task of being a single parent. She had a timid and nervous disposition and struggled to cope with having little money and no support. But I tried my best to welcome her, and we got on very well together. I soon learned all about her difficult childhood. When she was only eight, she had discovered her brother's body after he hanged himself in his bedroom and that awful experience understandably had a lifelong effect on her. I was forever lending her food, which I didn't mind at all, as long as she returned the favour when she was paid her social money. Tins of beans, loaves of bread, and boxes of eggs all seemed to be on a piece of elastic, continually borrowed and then returned across the fence.

One day we were chatting as we hung out the washing in our back gardens when I noticed something wrong with her face. I asked her to come closer, and could see that her features appeared to have drooped on one side as if she had suffered a stroke, although her speech was normal. I suspected she was suffering from Bell's palsy and told her she must see a doctor as soon as she could. I remembered a woman at the bus stop who had similar symptoms telling me that that's what she had been diagnosed with, and I hoped that it wouldn't cause Penny any permanent damage. Fortunately, she was able to be treated quickly – but it was months before her appearance was back to normal.

A little gang of the neighbourhood kids would regularly kick a ball or play tag together outside our front. During the holidays, as soon as they were old enough, Julie, Davie and Chris would head up Eston Hills with a gang of pals to explore the old mine workings, climb trees and swing on the home-made 'Tarzy' ropes up there. My only worry was that they might forget the time and not come home for their tea. When they returned they'd be dirty and tired, with grass-stained knees and clothes – but happy, and full of chatter about their adventures. I'd always ask them to pick some blueberries for me to put into pies and crumbles, and they usually came back with the plastic container full to the brim. But one time they returned empty-handed, declaring that the bushes were all bare and looking at me oh, so innocently – not realising their blue-stained lips and tongues gave the game away!

At Easter I boiled eggs for the kids to paint faces on and roll down the hill. It was one of the few times in the year when I would try to buy new clothes for them if I possibly could. Guy Fawkes' Night was another special occasion in our house. Our back garden was often chosen by the local youngsters to be the bonfire site, as we had no pets that might end up getting distressed or hurt, and the only plants that were going to be damaged in our yard were the weeds! Hardly anyone could afford fireworks, but if I managed to save a couple of bob I would buy a packet of sparklers for them to wave around and write their names in the night sky. I'd be busy all day making toffee dabs, peanut brittle and other treats, which only lasted a few minutes with our kids and their friends around. We usually had jacket potatoes with a sprinkle of salt and a huge knob of butter for tea – none of the fancy fillings we have today, but still delicious. Then it was time for apple-bobbing, and watching the kids half drown themselves trying to sink their teeth into one of the cheap Cox's I'd bought! The game usually ended in a riot of laughter, and they never tired of it. It was a wonderful time of year for the kids, just as Christmas was, and I loved seeing their smiling faces in the light of the bonfire, laughing and enjoying themselves without a care in the world. If only life could always be this way.

11

A Marriage Under Strain

As time went by, I realised that telling Kenny if the kids needed new clothes or shoes was pointless, because he wasn't interested. When the soles of their shoes wore thin and a hole appeared, I would cut out insoles from an old cardboard box to give me a few weeks' grace before I had to replace them. I used to make all their knitwear by hand, because it was more economical than buying jumpers and cardigans ready-made. When the option of purchasing clothes on credit with a 'Provvie' ticket became available, that's how I'd manage to buy the kids new school shoes, jeans and underwear. For every pound I borrowed, I paid a shilling a week to the man from the Provident when he called round to the house. Like most of the neighbours, as soon as one ticket was paid off I'd immediately take out another, because the kids always needed something.

This is an important part of women's work that people rarely think about. Anyone who tells you that working-class motherhood isn't an intellectually demanding job simply doesn't know what they are talking about. We aren't just busy shopping and cooking and washing – which anyone who's had children will tell you is hard physical labour, for a start. But there's also the mental load of calculating, forecasting, balancing and listing – to make sure everything is paid on time, and your budget stretches as far as you need it to. One day as a stay-at-home mam can be as chaotic and mentally draining as a day buying and selling shares in the City – only we aren't paid a penny for doing it!

Then there's the emotional side of caring for children (especially when your children are always in the wars, as mine were), which is never acknowledged as a serious skill. Outside our back door was a brick outbuilding that was supposed to be used for storing bikes and gardening equipment, although we didn't have either. The kids were told not to climb on the roof, but Davie – taking after me in his aptitude for balancing like a tightrope walker – never took any notice. One day he jumped down and slammed his chin on the wall, biting through the middle of his tongue as he did so. I dashed out of the back door after hearing his shouts and nearly fainted when I saw his mouth full of blood. The poor child couldn't speak and just looked up at me in terror, blood pouring down his front, but I couldn't find anything to stem the bleeding. Luckily for us – and maybe unluckily for her – a nurse lived a few doors down, at number one. She was used to being pestered by the mams when our kids had accidents. She took one look at Davie and told me not to waste my time taking him to the hospital because they can't stitch tongues. She said I should take him to the Paediatric Dental Clinic on Fabian Road, Eston, instead. The dentist there said she was right, gave me some mouthwash and told me to blend his food until the wound started to heal. Poor Davie's tongue had swollen up to three times its normal size and he couldn't speak properly for months afterwards.

Not long before this episode, we'd given Julie a pogo stick for Christmas. None of the other kids had one and they all queued up excitedly to see who could do the most hops before falling off. Davie had only managed two bounces when his feet slipped off the pedals and the pogo stick shot up and struck him square on the forehead, knocking him out cold. The other kids just stood around at first, wondering if he was playing possum. Chris started poking him with his toe and told him to stop messing around. When he didn't respond, Julie realised he was genuinely hurt and ran back into the house to tell me what had happened. Off we went for yet another trip to casualty – it's a wonder social services didn't come after me!

Chris had his fair share of being in the wars too. I was visiting Margie one day and left him and Davie playing outside her house. When I looked out of the kitchen window I saw that they had climbed on top of Arthur's car and were standing on the roof. The little monkeys were using it as a climbing frame. I banged on the window and shouted at them both to come down, but while Davie jumped off safely, Chris slipped and cracked his head on the pavement, resulting in a huge, egg-shaped 'keggy' on his forehead. I was horrified and carried him inside to put butter on it, which was supposed to help bring out the bruising, although thinking back it was probably just an old wives' tale. The poor kid was conscious, but concussed. As I didn't have the money for a trip to the hospital, I just had to keep a close watch on him. He soon recovered but the bruising on his head took weeks to fade away, and of course I blamed myself.

When he was only four or five, Chris went through a period of getting ugly carbuncles on his body. He developed a particularly large one on the back of his leg and I applied a soap and sugar poultice to draw out the infection. It was another old remedy but it seemed to do the trick. Within a day or two it was displaying a large head and was ready to be bathed and burst. But to do this I had to ask Julie to sit on his back while I washed the infected area, because he couldn't keep still and was shouting and screaming, poor kid. And poor Julie too! She was in tears because she felt so bad for holding him down – but if I hadn't cleaned it up, the carbuncle would only have returned and become worse. Most children suffered from boils at some time back then but it's not something you hear about nowadays, probably because kids have a much better and more varied diet with all the vitamins they need.

Incidents like these – which are an essential part of growing up – almost always require a mother's time and unique set of skills to help her kids bounce back. We supervise, we teach, we guide and when things goes wrong anyway, we're there to comfort, protect and heal. We're the ones who maintained life outside the drudgery of work so that the family had something worth coming back to – a friendly community and a loving, well-run household. Men like Kenny were oblivious to these aspects of parenting, and so those responsibilities landed squarely with us mothers. It was often thought at the time that women had the easier end of the deal – and when I think of all the horrors and accidents that happened at the various industrial sites, not to mention the squalid working conditions there, maybe we did in some ways. But our lives were far from the image of leisure and idleness that our husbands seemed to picture.

The cost of Kenny's bathing obsession continued eating into the household budget, but I still managed to carve out the time and money for some simple pleasures for myself when I could. Thursday was ladies' night in the Grangetown Legion Club, and if I had a couple of pounds to spare I looked forward to going out with the lasses and enjoying a game of bingo. I only had one or two half lagers, but it was the social interaction I went for. I'd become desperate for the feeling of normality I'd have when I was around my friends. Kenny hated me going anywhere. One Thursday the only decent outfit I owned went missing from the washing line. He said someone must have stolen it, but I wasn't stupid – why would they only take my clothes and leave everyone else's?

Going out to the club gave me a centre of gravity, because it confirmed that I wasn't crazy or unreasonable to expect some consideration and care from Kenny. The other girls' husbands might not have been perfect fathers, but their kids were their pride and joy, at least. My friends' eyes would light up as they talked about what they had done together as a family the previous weekend. For so long I'd believed that I should count myself lucky. At least Kenny wasn't a violent drunk. At least he wasn't a brute, as our ogre of a neighbour was. At least he didn't force me to do anything I didn't want to do – as my dad had done to my mam. It was fine to have standards for your other half, just as it was fine to have standards for yourself. But when I went out and mixed with other people, it reminded me that Kenny's detached and egotistical attitude simply wasn't normal any more, even if it might have been quite typical of the men of our parents' generation.

The other girls must have known something of how miserable my life with Kenny was, despite the fact that I tried hard to hide it. If I told them I couldn't afford to go out with them on a Thursday night, they would often coax me into joining them anyway, and even bought my drinks for me sometimes. When one of us won on the bingo or the raffle it was a major event for us all, although I only managed it three times in all my years of going to the Legion. I won a tray of pork chops, the two-bar electric fire that I once threatened to chuck into Kenny's bath, and – a fabulous luxury – a little black and white portable television that lived in our bedroom but moved all over the house, depending on who wanted to watch it.

One of my best nights out at the club was the time we went to see a hypnotist – a man dressed in a shiny, maroon suit, with an overly-coiffed hairstyle. He started by asking for volunteers to come up on stage with him and I was amazed to see how quickly some of them went under his spell. He gave each volunteer a different action to perform when a certain piece of music was played. One man transformed into a sergeant major whenever he heard God Save the Queen, jumping to his feet and marching around the room shouting commands and telling people off. When the hypnotist clicked his fingers the hapless man came to, bemused and bewildered as to why he was standing in the middle of a room of people who were roaring with laughter. One of my friends danced around like a ballerina, and another volunteer thought all the other men had stolen his ties and demanded them back. By the end of the act he was wearing about ten of them!

We laughed so hard that my face was aching all the way home as we relived the highlights together. I remember climbing into bed that night, pondering how the hypnotist had managed to persuade people to do whatever he wanted at the click of his fingers. If only I could do the same for Kenny, I thought. I would have given anything to snap him out of the unreachable place his mind was in. I couldn't let go of the thought and as I dwelled on it more and more over the next few days I came to wonder whether it was he who was the hypnotist and I who was the one leaping around the room acting the fool, playing all these ridiculous roles at his bidding. What would it take for someone to snap their fingers and bring me back to reality?

Kenny hurt me so deeply over the years that the love and affection I once had for him were gradually snuffed out. He seemed incapable of showing any consideration or kindness. My lovely kids kept me going, but Kenny's behaviour exhausted me, and I was under constant financial pressure. The stress of it all started to take a toll on my health. I was still only twenty-nine, when I found a lump in my breast as I was getting dressed one day. I was terrified. I knew several women who had had breast cancer, and was aware that it was often a death sentence in those days. What frightened me most of all was the worry of who would look after my kids if anything happened to me.

My doctor referred me to a specialist, who sent me to Eston Hospital to have the lump removed. Before the operation I had to sign the paperwork to say that if they found anything malignant they could remove my breast. After coming round from the anaesthetic, the first thing I did was look down to see if I still had two boobs. It was a huge relief to find that everything was present and correct, I can tell you. Even with my life in the balance, Kenny still didn't come to the hospital to see me, of course. But my sisters came – and even though she was only eight, Julie walked all the way to Eston on her own to visit me.

Julie was such a wonderful kid, always doing what she could to help at home. Kenny didn't trust banks, so he kept his money for cigarettes and beer hidden around the house. Julie hoovered all the bedrooms for me once a week and was a dab hand at finding shillings, or even the occasional half a crown, that he'd stashed away under the bedroom carpet, behind the chest of drawers or on top of the wardrobe.

'Just don't say anything to your dad,' I'd say when she handed over whatever she'd found. She never did tell him, of course, but eventually Kenny would storm down the stairs full of hell, demanding to know if anyone had found his money. I'd just smile and say, 'Finders keepers, losers weepers'. Then he'd storm off to lick his wounds, but I didn't feel guilty at all – we needed that money far more than he did.

Sunday February 14th, 1971, is a date etched in my memory. Not only was it our twelfth wedding anniversary, but it was also the last day when there were twelve pennies to the shilling, and twenty shillings to the pound. The next morning saw the dawn of Decimalisation Day, and the money we had grown up with was consigned to history. A pound was now made up of one hundred new pence, instead of 240 old pennies. We all found it difficult to adapt, and you often heard people asking shopkeepers, 'How much is that in real money?'

It was around this time that I started locking the back door and carrying a key for the first time in my life. Times were changing, and not everyone was as trustworthy and honest as they once had been. We were hearing more and more stories of burglaries and muggings and were being advised to take responsibility for our own safety by adopting certain precautions. That's how I came to lock myself out one time. Luckily, I'd left the small transom window of the toilet open, so I hitched up my skirt and climbed the waste pipe, then tried to wriggle myself through the tiny opening. I managed to squeeze the top half of my body in – no doubt showing the neighbours next week's washing in the process – but then I felt a searing pain in my right groin. I'd impaled myself on the solid metal window fastener, which stood about one-inch proud. I was well and truly stuck, dangling half in and half out of the window, high up on the outside of the house. After what seemed an eternity, I managed to free myself from the catch and slither head first downwards, only just avoiding landing in the toilet bowl. I was left with a nasty gouge and a large, painful bruise. Someone kindly pointed out later that I was lucky not to have severed an artery otherwise I'd probably have bled to death up there, which would hardly have been the most elegant way to go!

Burglars weren't the only bad boys to look out for – we also had a couple of peeping toms in the neighbourhood. One evening I was at the sink washing the pots after tea when I noticed the two lads who lived directly out of our back, Dougie and Ray, sitting at their bedroom window, apparently looking into my neighbour Barbara's house. After a while I became curious and went out into our garden to try to see what they were staring at. When I looked up, I could see Barbara's sixteen-year-old daughter Lily getting changed in her bedroom. I was furious, and went to see Barbara straight away to warn her. A few months later I was standing at the kitchen window again one sunny afternoon and saw Dougie standing at the end of his garden looking around furtively. He seemed to be unusually interested in Barbara's washing and I could see he was up to no good. As I watched, he jumped over the metal dividing fence into her garden and started gathering up Lily's pants and bras from the clothes-line, tossing the pegs onto the garden. I could hardly believe the cheek, and ran outside to confront him.

'What the hell do you think you're doing?' I shouted.

Dougie stood brazenly with one arm behind his back, hiding the underwear. I told him I'd seen everything and gave him the choice of pegging her clothes back or being reported to the police. He blushed scarlet as he bent down to pick up the pegs and reluctantly began returning the items to the line.

My three lovely children all enjoyed school and were always enthusiastic about it. I would sit and listen to them read in the evenings and tried my best to instil in them the importance of learning and getting all the qualifications they could. I loved spending as much time as possible with them at the weekend, and if Kenny wasn't at work I tried to persuade him to join in. Sometimes he would, but other times he just wanted to be left alone. He would go off for a walk on his own, usually to Eston Cemetery (he said he liked the silence there), or he would dig in the back garden, where he had started a vegetable plot.

On Saturday evenings the whole family would sit together to watch television and if Kenny wasn't working, he would join us. When I could, I'd buy a quarter of sweets to share out as a treat. One night, when I didn't have the money for sweets, I did my usual trick of placating the kids with cups of warm milk instead, which wasn't the same but it was cheap and kept them occupied. I happened to look across the room and noticed that Kenny was chewing away in the corner. For a moment I could only stop and stare, not quite believing what I was seeing. I asked him what he was eating and he admitted he'd bought himself some of his favourite Merry Maid toffees. I gazed at him in amazement.

'Haven't you bought the kids anything?' I asked.

Kenny just stared blankly.

'I didn't have enough money to buy them for everyone,' he said, and carried on chewing as he turned back to watch the TV.

I felt sick to my stomach, looking at this man who my children had to call their father. His handsome looks had long since faded. He sat there hunched over, an old miser chewing his sweets while the kids clutched their cups of milk right next to him. I could no longer see anything that redeemed him or justified the lifetime of drudgery I'd committed to in the service of his selfishness. Angry tears filled my eyes as I thought about all the times I had taught our kids to share everything they had with each other and with their friends – they were still in primary school and yet they would never have kept sweets to themselves when those around them had none. I thought about Julie's kindness when I had my cancer scare, and how an eight-year-old child had given me more support and comfort than my own middle-aged husband. I saw our lives ahead of us – how I would work myself into the ground to keep Kenny happy, and when I was too exhausted and worn down to do it any longer, he would start on Julie. She'd be made to step into my shoes to do everything for him out of guilt, simply because he would refuse to look after himself otherwise.

All of these emotions that had been building up for years rose to the surface at that moment and I blew my top with him, leaping out of my chair and calling him all the greedy bastards under the sun. As I screamed, hot tears streamed down my face. I hated the kids seeing me so upset, but it was a last, desperate attempt to shame him right there in front of them. But he simply shrugged, rolled his eyes, and carried on chewing his toffee. No amount of shouting, talking or crying would ever make him change. He was selfish to the core, and that was that.

12

Four Little Feet

The kids couldn't understand why I was spending so much time crying in the toilet. My periods hadn't stopped, so it was only when I noticed my clothes feeling tighter around my waist that I began to suspect I could be pregnant. I put it off for as long as I could, but a test at the doctor's eventually confirmed that I was expecting again – seven years after giving birth to Chris, our youngest. I loved having children, but we just couldn't afford another hungry mouth to feed. For a long time life had been an uphill struggle on Kenny's meagre wages, but I had recently found myself a little part-time job working as a cleaner. With Chris settled in primary school and old enough to dress and wash himself, at last there had been a glimmer of hope that we could finally lift our heads above water. And now this hammer blow.

I dreaded having to tell Margie the news. She was desperate to have a baby of her own and was going through all kinds of tests and procedures, but without success. And here I was, pregnant for the fourth time. I tried to pretend it wasn't happening for a few weeks, until the straining buttons across the front of my dress and my frequent dashes to the toilet made it obvious. When she figured it out, her face said it all.

'I don't understand why God has allowed you to fall pregnant again when you can barely afford to look after the three children you already have,' she said, unable to hold back her tears. 'I've been hoping and praying for a baby all these years, and I could give a child everything it needs...'

If only I could have transferred this new life growing inside me into Margie, I would have done it in a heartbeat. I didn't know why life had to be so unfair – but it was, and neither of us could do a thing about it. I just had to make the best of it and I tried to tell Margie that, but she was going through her own personal agony and it was hard for her to hear my explanations and if-onlys. It was devastating to know that my pregnancy was a source of pain to my wonderful sister, who had always been such a rock to me.

A few weeks later I was wearing a smock-type mac that hid my swelling bump, when a gypsy lady approached the queue at the bus stop on Birchington Avenue, selling little bunches of lucky white heather. I didn't have much money but everybody else turned their heads away so I handed over the few coppers in the bottom of my purse and smiled. She thanked me and took hold of my hand, looking me in the eye.

'You're pregnant,' she said. 'And you're going to have two babies.'

'I don't think so!' I blushed, and I thought little more of it.

In the weeks that followed, my bump grew so large that soon it was difficult to walk and I started getting terrible bouts of morning sickness. One day I was feeling unwell at the bus stop and a neighbour from round the corner saw me bent double, and rushed across to help. I was embarrassed that he'd noticed, but he insisted on knowing what the problem was. Before I knew it, he had gone for his friend and the two of them came back to help me, forming a chair out of their crossed arms with their hands joined together, and they proceeded to carry me home as though I was the Queen of Sheba! I nearly broke their backs as I was a fair size by now, but bless them, they were genuinely kind and caring, and I was grateful for their thoughtfulness.

I was never what you'd call petite, but by the time I was six months pregnant I was enormous. I was so round I had to waddle along holding my bump with both hands. The doctor suspected something wasn't right and sent me to the hospital. The gynaecologist there told me he could hear the baby's heartbeat but it was laid across my tummy, and if it didn't right itself within the next couple of weeks he would have to try to turn it. I came away inconsolable, just wishing my life could be straightforward for once.

Then one day in January 1972, I was shuffling slowly down to St Mary's School to collect Chris and Davie as usual. But as Chris came hurrying to meet me he stepped off the kerb to dodge a group of children between us, and to my horror he ran straight into the path of an oncoming motor scooter. He lay in the road badly dazed, although still conscious. The other children gathered round and stared. With nobody in sight who could help, I scooped my little boy up and carried him home myself. I should never have done it in my condition but I was determined to get him there. By the time we reached Deepdale Avenue I was fit to drop, but I could see that Chris was badly hurt so once I'd laid him gently on the settee I rushed off to the phone box to call an ambulance. X-rays revealed that his leg was broken. After a couple of hours we left the hospital but the cast weighed so much that poor Chris could hardly walk. Over the next few weeks his brother and sister tried their best to help, but I often had no choice but to carry him until the break had healed.

The following month I was with Margie at Normanby Top, on our way into Hinton's supermarket (one of the first shops in the area to be fitted with automatic doors). I don't know whether it was my enormous bulk or my slow pace that confused the mechanism, but the doors slid open to let me out and then slammed closed on my tummy as I tried to pass through. It must have looked almost comical at the time, but afterwards I felt a sharp pain inside. Not long after I returned home that evening I told Kenny what had happened and said I was going to bed early, as my back and tummy were aching. I woke up in agony in the early hours of the morning, and realised I had started to haemorrhage. I knew something was seriously wrong, because I had never experienced bleeding this heavy before and it was far too early for the baby to be coming. I woke Kenny and told him to ask my friend Sandra to come and sit with me, and then to go and call for an ambulance. I didn't want to wake the kids and let them see me in this state, but I didn't want to be left on my own either. My best nightie was already packed in my overnight hospital bag along with a few toiletries, so when Sandra arrived I must have looked a right state, wearing my old one with a nappy pin holding one shoulder up.

Kenny seemed to be gone forever but finally returned, followed shortly afterwards by the ambulance crew. It turned out that the phone box on Slater Road had been vandalised but Kenny had managed to flag down a police car and asked them to call an ambulance for me. I was mortified when the two paramedics said I had to sit on a rolled-up towel to help stop the bleeding while they carried me on a chair to the ambulance. The next thing I remember, I was lying high up on a bed in an examination room at Middlesbrough General Hospital. In front of me was a four-foot-ten Chinese doctor, asking if he could examine me. He produced a tape measure and threw it over my bulging tummy to measure my bump. I was in a state of shock having lost so much blood, and was terrified that I would lose my baby as well. I hadn't wanted another one, but after carrying it this long I already loved it and desperately wanted everything to be well. I was soon in for another shock.

'We need to x-ray you because the doctor thinks there must be more than one baby in there,' the nurse said.

As she spoke, I remembered what the gypsy at the bus stop had told me. Surely she couldn't have been right? The thought only added to my panic – how could we possibly cope with more than one baby? I barely had all the socks and booties we needed for two tiny feet, let alone four!

A portable x-ray unit was wheeled in and I was helped to lie face down on a stretcher with a large hole in the middle, into which they wanted me to position my bump. This was no easy feat as I could hardly breathe, let alone lie on my front. With the help of the nursing staff I finally managed, and within moments the doctor was able to confirm the news I was dreading.

'There's certainly more than one baby – and we need to bring them out straight away,' he insisted.

Cue pandemonium, with doctors and nurses rushing around as I was prepared for an emergency caesarean section. They must have knocked me out there and then because the next thing I knew I was coming to in a hazy beige hospital room, with blurry faces crowding around as the nurses tended to me. At first I couldn't remember anything at all and felt only a sense of drowsiness and a mild interest in the noises the nurse was making as she tried to speak to me. I nodded sleepily, without understanding anything she'd said.

'You have two gorgeous little boys,' the voice repeated, and this time I felt a pair of tiny faces being held against my two cheeks.

Rolf Harris' *Two Little Boys* was in the charts and the song kept playing in my head. But I was still too groggy from the anaesthetic to take in what was happening, and I quickly drifted back to sleep. When I awoke for the second time, the room was quiet. The nurse told me my twin babies had been born six weeks early and weighed just four pounds and a couple of ounces each. With no incubators available at the General, they had been taken by ambulance to North Tees Hospital in Stockton.

I was frantic with worry, and yearning to see and hold them. I was now wide awake but as I tried to sit up and protest, I felt a sharp, stabbing pain in my belly. I'd undergone a major operation and could hardly move. I knew Kenny wouldn't visit either me or the babies, seven miles away at North Tees, and I was desperate to be back home with my children.

That morning, Julie was awoken by someone hammering on the front door of our house. As she went down to see who it was she passed our bedroom, and noticed to her horror a huge blood stain on our bedsheets. The poor kid thought me and Kenny had been murdered in our sleep! She was already crying when she answered the front door, and it didn't help when she saw a stern-faced policeman looming over her on the doorstep. As her sobs intensified, he quickly explained what had happened during the night and that Kenny had gone to work for his six-till-two shift. He told her to dry her tears and take her brothers over to Aunty Margie's house. It was hard for an eleven-year-old to take it all in but being the sensible lass she was, Julie did as she was told and helped Davie and Chris dress for school before walking them up the road to Normanby.

Julie said Kenny looked bewildered when he turned up after his shift to take them home from school. She heard him tell Margie that he'd used the phone at work to call the hospital and when the nurse congratulated him on the birth of twin boys, he thought she had the wrong dad and put the phone down! He rang back and the same nurse answered again and assured him that she had the details right, and I definitely had delivered twin boys, because she'd seen them with her own eyes. She added that I was as comfortable as could be expected after having a C-section. Margie was as shocked as Kenny at this unexpected turn of events.

I was allowed to come home after a few days, and spent the following month begging and borrowing the bus fares to Stockton and back to visit my two beautiful little boys. I wasn't allowed to touch them but I spent hours gazing through the hospital screen at their tiny, vulnerable bodies, two sleeping baby birds in a nest, and I loved them with all my heart. We called them Ian James and Alan John, although I don't know where those names came from – we hadn't even talked about what we might call one baby, let alone two! When I wasn't at the hospital I would be knitting away furiously well into the night to make all the booties and cardigans I would need. A health visitor was assigned to visit our home to assess whether we required any assistance but I told her confidently that I could manage, and showed her the cabinet in our front room brimming with pairs of matching knitted baby clothes. We were also able to scrape together just enough money to buy a second cot, and a few other extra bits and pieces.

The day the twins came home was an ecstasy of joy and relief. I was still weak and shaky on my feet, but I beamed with pride at my little marvels. I hadn't even wanted one baby and yet having two felt like winning the pools. Ian and Alan might have been small but they were perfect in every way. Julie wasn't happy at first. She had wanted a sister and instead ended up with another two brothers to add to the two she already had. But her disappointment soon melted away as the babies won her heart, and she became extremely protective of her tiny new brothers – just as she was of Chris and Davie.

I felt so blessed to have five beautiful children. But the months that followed were some of the hardest of my life. When Kenny wasn't at work he spent hours on end in the bath. I had my work cut out with two new babies to look after, but still had to continue ferrying buckets of hot water up the stairs to him. Thank goodness I had Julie and the boys to help me. Julie became a second mam to the twins – at only eleven years old – and I wouldn't have been able to manage without her. She could wash, change and feed them as well as I could. The babies seemed to be able to survive without sleep and I was sometimes so tired that I gave the same hungry mouth both of the bottles I had prepared before going to bed, and then wondered why the other one was still crying. At times I resembled a zombie, after nights on end with just a few hours' sleep, but as the months went by they eventually settled into a routine and we all enjoyed some much-needed rest at last.

Chris was used to being the baby of the family and was more than a little jealous of the twins. On several occasions I had one of them on my knee, feeding or dressing him, when the poor baby's face would become contorted and he'd let out a piercing scream. When I turned my head, Chris would be either nipping the baby's finger or twisting a toe. He was always taking their dummies and hiding them or throwing them away. He even told me one day that he didn't want his new little brothers, and asked if we could send them back!

Ian reminded me of Julie when she was a baby, and he started crawling early. He could walk by the time he was nine months old, teetering left and right as me and the kids sat on the floor, squealing with excitement and encouraging him to come to us. Little Alan was more like Chris, and couldn't crawl or walk until he was nearly one. That was probably for the best though, as his brother turned out to be a little Houdini, and had to be watched like a hawk. Even when he was fastened into his side of the twin buggy, Ian still managed to free himself and wriggle out. Pushchairs had to be left outside shops in those days, and one day I came out after popping into Walter Baker's furniture store in Normanby for a couple of minutes to find Ian standing next to the pram! Luckily for me, he hadn't wandered off – he was probably trying to explain his escape plan to his twin and sure enough, it didn't take long before Alan was copying Ian's every move.

I can't remember who gave me the little wooden baby pen we had. It folded out into a square around four feet by four. I could put both babies in there with some toys and they were supposed to be safely contained – if only! It was hilarious to see Ian pull himself up the bars and then start to push the whole pen around the lounge. Poor Alan couldn't stand up yet and would end up being trailed around the floor like a doll on a conveyor belt!

One morning when the twins were around eighteen months old, I woke up at about five o'clock to the sound of running water coming from the bathroom. I got up to see what was going on and nearly died of shock to see them both sitting in the bath, fully clothed in their pyjamas and nappies, in ice cold water so deep it reached up to their chests. Their teeth were chattering and their lips were blue, but they were laughing and happily splashing around as though they were paddling on Redcar beach. They'd somehow managed to climb in and turn the taps on themselves. I plucked them out of the icy water as fast as I could, stripped their clothes off, wrapped them in towels, and put them in our bed to warm up. I used my own body heat to thaw them out, sick with worry that they might have caught a serious chill, but the boys just carried on giggling and thought it was all great fun.

Kenny was supposed to help me with the twins but usually managed to achieve the exact opposite, when he did anything at all. As far as he was concerned, duties were either my responsibility or his, with no grey areas. He never seemed to think he ought to step in when necessary, even if one of them had fallen over or hurt themselves. I remember walking in to see one of the babies sitting on the floor wailing, with a shocking bump on his forehead and Kenny sitting a few feet away in his armchair looking as if he hadn't a clue what to do. By this point he was so terrified of germs that he rarely touched the kids at all, especially if they had been at school or out playing anywhere. When I asked him how his child had bumped his head, he just shrugged.

'Haven't you been sitting here the entire time?' I asked him.

'Well, yeah, but I've been reading my paper,' he replied, as though that was an excuse.

The twins loved being bathed in front of the open fire and it was always a battle to get them out of the water afterwards. One cold winter evening when they were about two years old, I asked Kenny to fetch the baby bath while I got their pyjamas ready and then undressed them in the warmth of the glowing coals. They were standing naked waiting for at least ten minutes before their dad finally returned and plonked the baby bath down. I was disgusted to see that it only had an inch of water and a flannel in it.

'What the bloody hell is this?' I fumed.

He could go through gallons upon gallons of hot, soapy bathwater every week but expected his sons to be bathed in a little tepid water, in midwinter?

'Not happy? Well you can do it yourself then!' he snapped back.

Well, the red mist came down, and before I knew what I was doing I'd thrown the water all over him. What a sight! He was dripping wet – a cartoon character with the flannel hanging off his face, and the wallpaper behind him soaked apart from his outline. Typically, Kenny didn't react to being drenched and just strode off, grumbling to himself.

They say twins have a special bond with each other and my boys definitely did. They hated being apart even for a few minutes and couldn't bear not knowing what the other was doing. They did everything together and were always up to mischief. When one sat on the toilet, the other read a book on the landing outside the bathroom door until he had finished his business and then they swapped over. I put them to bed in their own bunks, but they always seemed to end up sleeping alongside each other in the same one. They enjoyed classical music, and would run around the lounge making a buzzing noise when I played *The Flight of the Bumblebee* on our record player. Whenever I could, I took them to Grangetown Library, just around the corner from us on Birchington Avenue. They loved spending time looking at what was available to borrow, and so did I. Reading was one of the few ways I could relax, so I was delighted to be able to borrow six books at a time. My worries about Kenny and his odd behaviour always seemed worse at night, and a good book was just about the only way I could switch off.

When the twins were three and a half, they were eligible to start nursery at St Mary's Catholic Primary School on Tennyson Avenue, which was where I had my little cleaning job. The fearsome Sister Apolline was my first headmistress there and her strict and sharp-tongued ways had the little ones quaking whenever she was nearby. But Mrs Devine, who took over when the old nun retired, was a lovely person and I'm proud to be able to call her my friend and colleague. I slogged my guts out washing the floors and scrubbing toilets, but I got a lot out of the job too. The other two ladies who worked with me would always make me laugh, and in our break times we enjoyed a nice cuppa together and a proper chin-wag. I was glad I could be so near to the twins when I was at work, after those awful early days in Julie's life when I had to run backwards and forwards to see her. I think it was reassuring for them too, knowing their mam was never far away.

Although my boys looked extremely alike, they weren't identical twins. 'Dizygotic', it's called – when two separate eggs are both fertilised at the same time. I never had any problem knowing which was which, of course, but then I'm sure that would have been the case even if they had been identical. Since the nursery teacher had so many other kids to look after she frequently mixed their names up, so I knitted them navy blue school jumpers with 'IAN' and 'ALAN' spelt out on the front. The first day they wore them, their teacher was delighted and she had no more problems telling them apart after that – although she still had an issue with them always wanting to see what the other one was doing in class! In the end, Mrs Devine decided to put them in different reception classes the following year. I was upset at first, knowing how devoted they were to each other, and how much they loved to be together. Mrs Devine was sympathetic, but she told me gently that they kept strolling across to check one another's work and it was disruptive both for each other and for their classmates. She explained that they would be able to see each other every playtime and dinner time, and that a few hours apart in between might help build their confidence. I understood her decision, and agreed that they would need to learn to be apart sometimes as they grew older.

Although Ian and Alan looked alike, in terms of personality they were completely different from each other. Ian was outgoing like me and loved performing and being the centre of attention. Ever since he was a baby, crawling around the room like a busy bumblebee, he was always in the thick of whatever was going on. But Alan was introverted and wouldn't initiate any trouble, although he was always quick to follow Ian's lead – which meant they often both ended up in bother for doing something they shouldn't have!

The miners' strike in 1972 had led to regular power cuts and made people realise just how reliant we were on coal. Not long afterwards, the council decided to upgrade the houses on our estate and take out the old coal fires, installing new gas fires and gas central heating instead. Oh, the sheer luxury of instant warmth in the winter months! We could hardly believe it, and the added bonus of plentiful hot water delighted me even more, as it cost far less to heat than our old system. The water for Kenny's interminable baths had been one of our biggest weekly expenses, and having access to such a cheap and convenient supply was an enormous relief. I found that I finally had the opportunity to enjoy my own baths, and could now afford to take ten minutes to soak away my aches and pains if I wanted to, instead of just dipping in and out as quick as a flash first thing in the morning.

With the passage of time, I adjusted to the way our life was, and stopped having to devote so much mental energy to just getting by. We still didn't have much in the way of material possessions, but I was always perfectly content as long as my bairns were. I'd like to think they had a happy, loving, normal childhood – or as normal as is possible when you grow up thinking your dad lives in the bath, at least.

13

—·—

THE MOST WONDERFUL TIME OF THE YEAR

C hristmas was the highlight of the year for my kids, and it was usually the only time they received new toys. I was determined to make it special for them and would start putting money aside months beforehand so they would all have something exciting to open on Christmas day. But it was a stressful time too, because Kenny had no interest at all in Christmas, and we always ended up arguing if he wasn't at work on Christmas morning.

I don't understand why he would want to spoil that day, of all days. Perhaps it was because he was never given anything for Christmas himself when he was a child, banished to his grandparents' house, and he just didn't know how to celebrate it – I don't know, he never told me. But in the middle of all the kids' delight on Christmas morning, he would just look around at their presents and fret about how I'd managed to pay for them all. It was as if Scrooge had turned up to mar our family's Christmas joy.

I was able to afford the presents because I was lucky enough to have a friend who was a catalogue agent. I would select toys from the catalogue in August and start to pay back small amounts every month to have a few gifts put away for the kids in time for Christmas, all hidden out of sight in the loft. I made sure they each had a main present (a game or a scooter, for example) along with a few little extras such as colouring pens and books. As well as buying their presents from the catalogue, I would also order clothes for them - one month it would be something for Julie, and the next would be the lads' turn. I'll be forever grateful to that friend. I tried never to miss a payment, but on a couple of occasions when I was in dire straits she helped me out by covering the instalment for me until I could pay her back – I don't know what I would have done without her.

I wanted Christmas to be a wonderful time for us all and I loved sharing the kids' excitement on Christmas morning, but if Kenny was around he would just ignore the pleasure on their faces and shoot me a look of disgust.

'Where did the money for all this come from?' he'd want to know.

He hadn't realised that I was using the catalogue to buy presents, and he'd play hell over it. And so it was that some years the kids would spend Christmas day listening to their dad berate me, as they played silently with their toys amid the angry voices.

In 1973, when David was nine, I bought him a red Raleigh Chopper for Christmas – and boy, was it well used! The distinctive bike was all the rage at the time, with its extended motorbike-style silver handlebars, long black seat and big back wheel. Davie and Chris would take turns each to pedal while the other was given a 'croggie', as we always called it. You had to change gear using a lever on the crossbar, which might have looked impressive but wasn't the cleverest place to put it, and the lads regularly fell forward and hurt their bits and bobs – it's a miracle they didn't do themselves a permanent mischief!

Kenny was forever pinching the Chopper to take the twins out for some fresh air, because he didn't like pushing their twin buggy. He would sit one of them facing forwards on the crossbar where the gear lever used to be (it eventually broke, so he'd removed it to avoid injuries), with the other one facing backwards on the long seat with him. A grown man with two small children on one exceedingly odd-looking bike was a striking sight as he cycled through the streets of Grangetown! He was supposed to take them to the park so they could play on the swings and slides, but I don't think he ever did. Instead, he'd head over to his beloved Eston Cemetery, where he appreciated the peace and quiet and said he could let them run around without any worries. Friends were always telling me they'd spotted the twins playing in and out of the gravestones, but no matter how I asked, begged or pleaded with Kenny not to take them there, he never took any notice. I wouldn't have minded if he had taken them to the park occasionally at least – but no, he preferred the cemetery, although I thought it was a strange place to take two little boys to play.

The kids and I made the most of any opportunity to play games together, and we spent many enjoyable hours every Christmas getting to grips with whatever new activities they'd been given in their stockings that year. Snakes and Ladders, Frustration, Kerplunk and Mrs Potato Head were all great favourites of ours. We also had a family tradition of playing Old Maid, but only ever at Christmas – I don't know why we never played it at any other time of year!

Kenny made no effort to share our Christmas happiness, he just seemed to focus on the money I'd spent. There were two particularly upsetting Christmases that stand out for me, when sadly it was our Julie who bore the brunt of Kenny's unreasonable reactions. On both occasions he made such a fuss that she ended up in tears.

The first was around 1974, when she would have been thirteen or so. I'd managed to buy her a brand-new, gold-coloured bicycle and she was completely surprised and over the moon with it. Unfortunately, as soon as Kenny saw the bike he became furious with me and started ranting on again about the money I'd borrowed. He was obsessed with the idea of debt (never having needed to borrow any money himself of course, because he had me to do that for him). Julie was so upset at the trouble she thought she'd caused that she told me later she wanted me to send the bike back. I eventually managed to talk her round and explain how much I wanted her to keep it. But I was so angry with Kenny for his meanness. All that work scrimping and saving to see our daughter's face light up on Christmas morning, just to watch as Kenny spoiled it for her! The fact was, I never did find myself in serious debt, and Julie loved that bike. She had years of pleasure riding it around the estate, and I will always be proud of that.

Kenny managed to ruin another Christmas for our daughter a couple of years later. Julie had asked for one of those portable record players that pack up like a little suitcase, with the speakers in the lid and a carrying handle. I found one but didn't have the cash to buy it outright, so this time I signed up for the buy-now-pay-later scheme at the Co-op on Eston High Street. It was exactly what she'd wanted, but as soon as Kenny saw it he kicked off again and started grousing about me always being a borrower and not being able to live within my means.

'What on earth do you owe for that? You must be up to your eyeballs in debt! Well, when the bailiffs turn up they can take you to jail, because your reckless spending is nothing to do with me.'

He spat out the word 'debt' the same way he did the word 'dirt', as though it was so contaminated and disgusting that he couldn't even bear to utter it. Well, it was true – I did have debts. When you live on a pittance, you do what you have to do so your children can have the memories you never had yourself. I always made the payments on time, and was never in all my life blacklisted or made bankrupt. If debt was the only way I could buy the kids what they needed, then so be it. Unlike Kenny, I certainly didn't see it as a shameful thing that tarnished the people who had to make use of it – for me, and for most of the women I knew, debt was a way of life.

Poor Julie was scared to death when she heard Kenny's warnings about me being thrown into prison and having nothing to do with me if I didn't make the payments. She thought I was going to be locked up and it would be all her fault. Once again, I had to reassure her that she had nothing whatsoever to worry about. Life was hard enough for my kids, knowing how different our home was from the relaxed and tranquil households that most of their friends were brought up in. Whatever it took, I was determined to do everything I could to make them happy – and I was going to make damn sure they had what they wanted for at least one day in the year!

14

MONEY LAUNDERING

Kenny continued to scrub himself for hours every day, until he developed a painful psoriasis condition. Angry red patches appeared all over his skin, especially on his knees, elbows and ankles, but he still refused to see a doctor. I worried that he would end up with a serious skin infection, but nothing I said made any impression on him. Sometimes the affected areas would crack and break open, leaving weeping, ugly sores. I was forever trying to find the best creams and lotions to treat him, but they were expensive and none of them seemed to make much difference as long as he continued with the prolonged and repeated scouring.

I was also concerned about the effect all this was having on the children. When they were little they didn't question what he did – I suppose kids think whatever happens at home is normal. As they grew older, I tried my best to shelter them from his peculiarities, but it became increasingly difficult. I didn't want them to see how sick their dad was, and tried to hide as much as I could from them, but eventually I gave up – they could see it for themselves.

I know Kenny loved the kids in his own way, but thanks to his own lonely upbringing he had no idea what to do with them or how to display emotion or affection. They didn't like to be left alone with him and Julie complained that he was always nagging at them to wash their hands. The crunch came when he tried to wash the kids the way he washed himself. I was out at the shops one day when he took Julie, Davie and Chris up to the bathroom and told them he was going to clean their hands because they were dirty and they didn't know how to wash themselves properly. As I opened the front door I heard a ruckus coming from upstairs, so I hurried up to see what was going on.

'He's saying we're dirty and we're not!' Julie protested.

I was livid. It was bad enough that he was harming himself through his paranoid habits, but I certainly wasn't prepared to stand by and watch him brainwash the children into adopting his unhealthy obsessions.

'If you ever try a trick like this again, I swear I'll drop the electric fire into the bath while you're in it!' I threatened.

For once, he seemed to take my words seriously and as far as I know that was the last time it happened.

However, Kenny's own bathing continued to spiral from excessive to downright disturbing. As his routine grew longer and longer (as I said, it could take up to four or five hours an evening), he was soon using a whole bar of soap every day. But it still wasn't enough for him. He became convinced that the door handles were harbouring millions of harmful germs. Once he was out of the bath, he would walk around the house with his hands jammed in his pockets, refusing to touch anything for fear of becoming tainted. If he couldn't persuade one of the kids to open the living room door for him, he'd take his foot out of his slipper, lift his leg, and pull the handle down with his toes – often looking as though he was about to topple over in the process. I hated it when he did this in front of the children, because I didn't think it was healthy for them to have to witness such a bizarre performance from their father.

Knowing how I felt about his behaviour, Kenny became more adept than ever at keeping secrets from me - and as his compulsions grew more extreme, his secretiveness only increased. Returning home from a day out with Julie and Ian, I found him busy fixing new handles on the two downstairs doors. It wasn't like him to take on DIY jobs, and the handles were perfectly all right when we'd left that morning.

'What's going on?' I asked, but he just continued screwing the handles on without answering or even looking up.

I huffed and went into the kitchen to make a cup of tea, and there I discovered that we had also acquired a new teapot and cups. The perfectly good ones I'd used that morning were nowhere to be seen. I was too tired to butt heads with Kenny when I knew I wouldn't be given a straight answer anyway, but I struggled to come up with any reasonable explanation for all this.

'Do you know what that was about?' I asked Chris, as I tucked him in to bed in that night.

He shook his head, but I could see he knew more than he was letting on because he wouldn't look me in the eye. I didn't push him, I merely raised my eyebrows in expectation as he shifted uncomfortably, until his face finally crumpled.

'Dad sent me out with a list of the things he said were contaminated,' he told me, close to tears.

It soon emerged that this was by no means the first incident – in fact it had happened so many times over the past year that the assistant at the hardware shop in Eston had asked Chris what on earth he was doing with all the door handles. He couldn't tell me exactly how many he'd bought, but it seemed to run into the dozens. They had a regular routine, often triggered by a visitor coming into the house or an event that had upset Kenny. Chris said his dad would give him a screwdriver to take the old, contaminated handles off, and then Kenny would put the new ones on himself.

I shouldn't have been shocked by this escalation in Kenny's illness, but I was. I couldn't believe that on top of the heating and the water and the soap, he was now squandering money on completely unnecessary new door handles when we couldn't even afford basic necessities for our kids. What made me even angrier was the fact that Kenny had sworn Chris to secrecy, making him lie to me and putting him in an impossible position, stuck in the middle between his parents. That was something I was not prepared to tolerate.

Kenny's behaviour continued to become more and more extreme. If he went somewhere in his normal clothes and felt he'd come into contact with somebody or something he considered to be unclean, he would bin all of his clothes as soon as he arrived home and then jump straight into the bath. I spent weeks knitting him a lovely jumper for Christmas one year and when I asked him where it was a couple of weeks later, he wouldn't answer.

'Please don't tell me you've got rid of it,' I said.

'I don't know where it's gone!' he blustered.

But I knew. He'd thrown it away.

Worse was to come when Kenny got it into his head that the money he brought home in his weekly wage packet was contaminated with the dirt from the steelworks, and he began taking the banknotes and coins into the bath with him. I was horrified the first time he handed me a pile of wet one- and five-pound notes for my housekeeping.

'What the hell am I supposed to do with this?' I asked.

Talk about money laundering! I persuaded the cashier at the Yorkshire Bank in Eston to exchange my soggy notes for new ones by telling her I'd mistakenly washed them with our clothes. It worked well enough the first time, but when I tried it again a couple of weeks later one of the clerks recognised me and I could see them whispering behind cupped hands, clearly thinking I was trying to pull a fast one.

As the ritual continued over the months that followed, I tried every way I could think of to dry out the notes before I dared take them to the shops. I spread them out on a baking tray and put them in the oven, which from the other side of the glass door seemed to be working, until they came out with their edges singed. Later, I came up with the idea of ironing them on a cool setting, placing them between two tea towels and then leaving them spread out on the kitchen table to dry overnight.

Kenny's refusal to seek help for his condition, and his denial that he even had a problem, had already ground me down long ago. Now it was grinding the kids down too. It was always them and me who ended up bearing the brunt of Kenny's OCD, as we had to go out and face the world while he stayed inside, hiding himself away. I once read that a husband and wife should be like a pair of trees growing alongside each other – independent, but both growing upwards with the same purpose and determination to reach the sky, sharing the soil they stand on and winding their branches together over time. My marriage with Kenny was more like a river, flowing freely and happily until a giant boulder rolled down and came to rest right in the middle of it: immovable and awkward and ever-present. My life, and the kids' lives, could still flow around the boulder to some degree, but as Kenny's illness got worse the obstacle grew ever larger and our waters became stagnant. The stress of living in our house was causing the older kids to squabble far more than they ever used to, probably following our lead. We reached a crossroads when Julie plucked up the courage to talk to her dad and try to explain how hard the situation was for all of us. That night I finally managed to persuade him to see a doctor. I made the appointment for him and when the day arrived I went with him, trying to be as supportive as I could.

'You'll feel so much better once someone understands what you've been going through,' I assured him. 'It must be hard having to bottle everything up inside, but the doctor will know exactly what to do.'

When we arrived at the waiting room, Kenny told me sharply that he didn't want me to go in with him to see the GP, so when his name was called I sat down to wait. I absent-mindedly picked up a magazine, trying hard not to worry about what was happening on the other side of the door, and praying that there might at last be some light at the end of our long, dark tunnel. But I had barely started reading when Kenny came marching back out, muttering under his breath. I had to jog a little to catch up with him outside the surgery, and I asked him what was the matter. He whirled around, his eyes full of fury.

'There's nothing wrong with me, see – and if there is, then it's your fault, you stupid woman!' he snapped.

We were in the middle of the street and people at the nearby bus stop were staring over to see what the commotion was. Kenny stormed off home on his own as I stood and stared blankly after him, knowing that persuading him to see a doctor had been my last hope, and it had failed.

After that, talking to him was pointless. He'd just stand up and walk away whenever I tried to bring up anything of any importance. I never did find out what the doctor said to him that day – but whatever it was, it did absolutely nothing to help any of us. In the end, I gave in to the deep resentment and frustration that had taken root between us. I'd always rested my hopes on him being diagnosed and treated, but it finally hit home that that was not going to happen. By now he was simply too ill.

15

— · —

SCRAPES AND TRANSGRESSIONS

W e were always taking one step forward and two steps back when it came to money. We weren't the only ones – most families were in the same boat as us – but finding ways to make whatever we had last until the next pay-day now dominated my life. In the evenings, me and the kids often sat talking or playing games illuminated only by the streetlamp outside, because I didn't have the two-shilling coins I needed for the electric meter – even when Kenny was out, and I was allowed to go into the cupboard. It would usually mean an early night for us all, but at least I can hold my head up and say I never resorted to raiding the coin box and pinching back the cash, as many people did. Talk about robbing Peter to pay Paul!

Even though the school and the parish priest knew fine well that most families had nothing to spare, it didn't stop them from putting pressure on the parents by constantly asking for money. The kids were forever coming home from school pestering me for donations to one charity or another. The biggest fundraiser of them all was when they decided they needed a church for Whale Hill, the new estate springing up just beyond Eston. We already had St Mary's, a beautiful old church in Grangetown where families had worshipped for generations, but that wasn't enough for the bishop and he wanted another. Each of my kids was issued with a payment card and told they had to 'buy a brick', piling the guilt on those whose mams didn't have enough to pay up. I barely had enough money to feed my family, never mind any extra cash to help build their blooming church. I'd seen postcards of St Peter's Basilica and other grand Catholic cathedrals - enormous buildings encrusted in gold – why couldn't they use some of that money to build a church over here in Middlesbrough? And while Kenny had insisted the kids were brought up Catholic, he never parted with a penny of his own to help them buy their precious bricks!

Not long after St Anne's was paid for and completed, they decided St Mary's was beyond repair and had to be pulled down. The priest moved out and the place was left derelict. It became a target for vandals, who gradually stripped away its precious treasures – all paid for by the sweat of Grangetown's poor. Nothing was too big or too sacred to be a target. Julie came home one night saying she'd seen the police chasing some kids along Bolckow Road after they'd broken in and tried to make off with the Stations of the Cross.

Kenny had made an effort to grow vegetables in our back garden, which would have saved us a few pennies on the groceries, but sadly only the slugs and caterpillars ever tasted the cabbages and cauliflowers he sowed. His solitary success was growing enough new potatoes for a couple of nights' tea. Then one hot summer's day he burned his back badly while gardening without his shirt on. Some clown at work told him the best remedy was a steaming hot flannel on the burnt area, and no matter how much I tried to tell him it was a bad idea, he wouldn't listen. He always knew better than I did. So he went ahead, and we had to watch him dance around the kitchen in agony after making a painful burn even worse.

Our back garden was always something of an embarrassment. It was a good size, but instead of flowerbeds and a lawn we just had flattened mud and a straggly assortment of weeds. We could never afford to do anything with it, but when the twins were about two years old, Kenny grew sick of me moaning about it being an eyesore and he bought a large bag of grass seed. In fairness, he did a decent job and within no time the whole place was covered in lush green grass. It was hard work keeping the kids from trampling on it while the seed took root, but it was worth the effort. For the first time since we'd moved in as the original tenants in the early sixties, the garden was presentable.

What a shame it didn't last! After a few months, the lawn was beginning to look overgrown so Kenny borrowed a lawnmower from a neighbour for its first cut. It didn't go well. The mower was so old and the cutting blade so blunt that the grass was pulled up at the roots. Within a few weeks we were back to flattened mud, and after that Kenny more or less hung up his spade for good.

When we first experienced the luxury of having a fitted carpet instead of just a rug over the lino, it felt wonderful. The only trouble was that the lounge doors would no longer open and close without catching on the thick pile. It was typical of Kenny never to ask for my opinion or consult me on anything, so his solution was to wait until I was out of the house, then take a hacksaw and cut the bottom off the doors. What a mess he made of it, though! The gap was wide enough to drive the kids' Matchbox cars underneath, and in the winter a gale-force draught blasted right through the room.

Sunday was my favourite day of the week. I'd set the table and we'd all sit down to eat Sunday dinner together as a family, even if we often had to make do with mince rather than a proper joint of meat. The kids always bolted their food if any roast potatoes were going spare. For tea we had jelly and ice cream, with bread and butter to fill up on, and a few cakes and biscuits when I could afford them. After tea, we would perform our usual variety show, and as soon as they were old enough the twins loved to join in too – with Ian leading the way and little Alan following along.

Emulating their older siblings, the twins were always getting into scrapes. I was in the kitchen doing the weekly wash one Monday when I heard a bloodcurdling scream coming from outside. I didn't recognise the voice at first, but mother's intuition told me it was one of mine and I darted out of the back door, still wearing my slippers. The racket was coming from Sandra's back garden, next-door-but-one, and without a second thought I hurdled the fence to find our little Ian (he'd be about five at the time) standing on top of an old wardrobe that had been left lying on its back, with his finger trapped in the door jamb. It was easy enough to free him, once I lifted him off the door, but the sight of his poor little finger as flat as a pancake was enough to turn my legs to jelly. It still hadn't returned to its normal size after I gently cleaned and bathed it, so it was time for another trip to Middlesbrough General. It was only as we were leaving the hospital, after Ian had been treated, that I noticed the four-inch gash in the bottom of my own foot. In all the commotion I hadn't realised I'd cut myself as I leapt to his aid. What a life! We never had a boring minute, I can tell you.

The Legion trip continued to be the highlight of our summer. One year they took us on our first visit to the lovely seaside town of Seaburn, near Sunderland. We set off in a chain of clapped-out coaches on one of those burning hot sunny summer days that we only seemed to have in the 1970s. Once we reached our destination, all the mams set out our deck chairs on the beach and laid down towels in front of us for the kids to sit on. The tide was out when we arrived, so the little ones stripped off to their underwear and immediately scampered away to paddle in the sea. I relaxed and chatted with the girls as I watched Julie disappearing with the twins and the others, all of them dancing and jumping in excitement as they neared the water's edge. The kids returned wet and sandy after half an hour or so, but as we counted them back I realised Alan was missing. With so many people on the beach I was frantic with worry and started shouting his name, fearing that someone might have snatched him. Together with some of the other women I began searching desperately for him, dashing in and out of deck chairs, oblivious to the sand I was kicking into the other day-trippers' picnics. After what seemed an eternity – but was, in fact, just thirty minutes – we found Alan playing happily with another group of families. He had wandered back up the beach on his own but veered off too far to the right and missed us. It brought back traumatic memories of our Julie wandering out of my sight when she was a toddler – what is it about kids and beaches! I was dothering like a leaf and my friends insisted that I sit down to have a cigarette and some sweet tea, and that traditional remedy for shock seemed to calm my nerves.

After a lunch of warm but welcome sandwiches it was time for the kids to head over to the funfair. The Legion had given them each a booklet of free tickets and they were eager to try out the rides. I wanted to go with them but the other mams insisted they would be fine on their own, since the fair was right next to the beach. So once again the gang set off, Julie promising me she would hold the twins' hands and only go on the little 'uns rides with them.

They had been gone just a few minutes when they returned and I could see straight away that something was badly wrong. Julie was carrying Ian in her arms and blood was pouring from a large gash above one of his eyes. I leapt to my feet but must still have been shaken from the upset of losing Alan. The next thing I knew, I was waking up in the First Aid tent. I looked around and saw that I was laid out on one stretcher, and Ian was beside me on another. Julie had forgotten to fasten his seatbelt on the bumper cars and he had lurched forward and banged his forehead when they slammed into another car. The trip we'd looked forward to for weeks had turned into a nightmare and I just wanted to go home, but we had hours to wait until it was time for the buses to return. I've never been so glad to see Grangetown and my own house as I was that evening!

Another time, Ian could have lost a couple of toes when a heavy iron drain cover dropped onto his foot. The twins had been playing just outside our house and managed to prise the lid open and lift it up. When a concerned neighbour shouted to ask what they were up to, Alan panicked and dropped his side of the cover straight onto Ian's toes. He was lucky to be wearing strong wellies and escaped with just bruising, but he walked with a limp for several days afterwards.

Despite these mishaps, they were well-behaved kids and never brought any real trouble to our door – though they did end up in a few sticky situations as they grew older, as most of us do when we're finding our way in the world. When Julie was sixteen I asked her to take Davie and Chris to Reeds in Eston to buy them new school trousers, while I stayed at home with the twins. I'd promised the older boys a fashionable pair of Oxford bags with a square patch pocket on the outside of the leg like the ones their mates were wearing. Once they'd tried some on and decided which ones they liked, Julie joined the queue at the till to pay. Davie said he needed the loo and headed out to use the back alley, but as he opened the shop door, a loud alarm started blaring. The shop assistant leapt from behind the till and grabbed Davie's arm, asking him what he had taken. Julie thought there must have been some mistake, and was shocked when he opened his jacket pocket without answering and produced an elastic snake belt, with the large plastic tag still attached. All three of them were ushered into the storeroom and the assistant locked the door while she called the police. Julie couldn't understand why Davie would do such a thing. The only answer she could prise out of him was that the kids at school were taking the mickey because they had all been shoplifting and said he was too chicken to try it. Whether it was peer pressure or bullying, it didn't matter, the damage was done.

The first I knew about it was when the police car pulled up outside our house. I was shocked to see the three of them inside and even more upset when the police officer explained what had happened, and said Davie and I would have to go with him to South Bank Police Station. Davie had always been such a quiet kid, and was the last little boy in the world you would expect to end up in trouble with the police.

I'd never even set foot inside a police station before. There seemed to be locks on every single door. At first Davie refused to say anything, but I eventually managed to persuade him to tell the truth and explain to the policeman why he had taken the belt. It struck me that his dad had never been made to take responsibility for his actions when he'd stolen the bookie's money all those years ago, and it might have been better for him if he had. Davie looked relieved to make a clean breast of it and after a couple of hours the sergeant said they'd be in touch to let us know if he would have to go to court, and he was released.

The poor lad didn't speak for a week afterwards, he was so badly affected by the whole affair. I was thoroughly ashamed at first and struggled to understand what we'd done wrong for Davie to decide to steal, especially when I was already treating him to the trousers he wanted. I worried that we'd failed somehow as parents. Maybe I hadn't protected him well enough from the bullies at school – and because of that, he was going to have a criminal record.

In the days that followed I convinced myself that they would send him away to prison, and I was haunted by images of his forlorn little face looking out at me as he gripped his cell bars. By the time the letter from the sergeant arrived I was in a right state, and my hands shook uncontrollably as I opened the envelope. I can't describe the relief I felt when I read the words 'juvenile caution'. As a result of the panic and anxiety, my newly-permed hair turned as straight as an arrow. (It was months before I could afford to have it done again – just my luck!)

Davie had never been in any kind of trouble before, and the only subsequent incident occurred one time when he was accused of smashing an electrical socket cover in the lads' toilets at St Peter's Secondary School. He came home sheepishly one night with a letter, which Julie noticed him trying to hide away in his jacket pocket. She asked him what it was, and when he finally produced it I saw that it was a note from his headmaster asking me to go into school to discuss something that had happened.

'Come on, tell me all about it,' I sighed.

Davie explained that a teacher had walked in while he was washing his hands after using the toilet. Another four boys were also in there with him. The teacher noticed the broken socket and asked which of them had done it but all five denied any knowledge. Of the five mams who received the letter, I was the only one who bothered to attend the school to talk about the matter. The head knew Davie and believed he was telling the truth. He thought it was more likely that responsibility lay with one of the other lads, whose parents hadn't even thought it worth responding to his invitation.

A major mistake I made when our Chris was a youngster was letting him have a hamster. The kids all wanted to play with him and were forever taking the little trembling creature out of his cage to pet him. Once, he managed to wriggle free and before we knew it he'd scrambled inside the frame of the settee and try as we might, we couldn't tempt him out again. We could hear him rustling around for days until he finally managed to escape and emerged into the daylight – the poor thing must have been starving.

Some months later, Chris said he thought the hamster had something wrong with him. When I went to look he was curled up, stock still, in the corner of his cage. I don't know why, but for some reason I decided to give him a drop of sherry. I suppose I thought it might perk him up. Well, it certainly did – for a little while, at least. He went into overdrive and began running around his wheel as if he was possessed! The next morning I found the poor little thing lying dead among the sawdust in the bottom of the cage. I felt terrible. How was I going to explain to Chris that my cure had killed his beloved pet?

Our first-ever family holiday was in 1978, when we spent a wet week in a caravan at the top of the cliffs near Whitby Abbey. We went for a ramble every day and returned to the caravan tired and soaked to the skin, before spending the evening listening to more rain batter the caravan roof. I struggled to dry our clothes overnight, ready for the next day's activities – but the kids thought it was all an adventure. On one of the days, Kenny decided we should walk over to Robin Hood's Bay, but it took longer than anticipated and by the time we arrived it was dark. We didn't have any money for a bus back, so we had no option but to return to the caravan on foot, through the fields in the pitch black – which was pretty hairy, with five kids! Then on our last day we went out for a stroll along the edge of the cliffs near the caravan park. Kenny warned the children several times not to touch the electrified safety fence but unfortunately Alan couldn't resist the temptation, and reached out before I could stop him. Luckily for him, he was wearing wellies, so when he touched the wire the shock went straight through him – and into Kenny, who was holding his hand. The poor man almost bit through his pipe and his left arm and leg shot out, just like the comedian Harry Worth doing his trademark star jump optical illusion (if you're old enough to remember that!). Kenny was fine, though far from amused, but the sight of his hair standing on end made it hard for the rest of us to keep a straight face.

Because Thursday was Kenny's pay-day, I'd set off every Friday to the Walter Wilson superstore on Fabian Road for my weekly shop, and then haul four or five carrier bags of shopping for the twenty-minute walk home, sweating cobs the whole time. My arms would feel as if they had stretched another foot in length by the time I finally arrived back and experienced the ecstasy of letting the bags drop to the floor, then I'd summon the kids to put down their skipping ropes or leave their footballs and come and give me a hand. They all became wonderful little helpers once they were old enough to know where to put the packets and tins, and they enjoyed coming along to the supermarket with me. Well, most of the time, at least.

One year I was getting the big Christmas shop but they were having fun playing in the street, so I asked them to follow along in a few minutes and meet me when I'd finished shopping. They all agreed, but by the time I'd loaded up my bags at the checkout there was still no sign of any of them, so I had no choice but to set off on my own. I was soon exhausted from the strain of carrying the bags, and I needed to stop several times to catch my breath and let the circulation return to my fingers for a few blissful seconds before setting off again. The flush in my cheeks by the time I turned the corner into our avenue was pure anger. The kids spotted me and I could tell by their faces that they'd clean forgotten and knew I would be far from happy with them. That was putting it mildly – I was bloody fuming! They all ran up, full of apologies and offers of help.

'You're too late to help me now,' I said as I swung the shopping bags to shoo them away with the last of my strength, even though my arms had turned to jelly. I was in a bad mood for a little while, banning them from the kitchen while I tidied everything away, but I soon softened later on when they all made such an effort to make it up to me. Julie supervised Davie and the twins while they helped her prepare dinner, one of them peeling spuds while the others chopped carrots and a head of cauliflower. Chris brought me a lovely cup of tea (a deep golden colour, just how I like it) while I relaxed on the sofa, and I ended up cuddling them all and telling them what a daft bunch they were. I could never stay angry with them for long.

Many years later, when the kids were grown up, they ferried me back and forth to the shops in their cars as often as I wanted, so they've more than made up for it since. I wonder if their kind offers of help were ever prompted by guilty memories of that day!

16

ALL SAINTS DAY

E verything changed on All Saints Day, 1979. We'd all enjoyed the fun of Halloween the night before, carving turnips to make into lanterns, as we always did. The next day was a Holy Day of Obligation for Catholics, when all the children were expected to go to Mass. Instead of walking the twins to school that morning I took them to St Anne's, the new church on Birchington Avenue that we'd scrimped and saved to help pay for. It was a bright, chilly day, and the boys were in high spirits as they kicked the piles of red and brown leaves around the pavement. They were delighted to meet up with their classmates and hardly noticed me leaving them when I slipped into a bench at the back of the church, after deciding to stay for the service. The children were all lined up in front of the altar and the organ began to play a stirring hymn. Even though I'm not Catholic, I loved sitting and listening to the children singing, their voices ringing out sweetly as the music echoed around the bright, modern church. I watched the twins standing side by side, focusing so seriously on the back wall of the church as they tried to make sure they remembered the right words. My heart swelled with pride when they finished the final hymn, then all the kids beamed proudly and looked around to try to spot their parents and give them a little wave. Afterwards the parish priest, Father Brennan, gave the blessing and the teachers lined the children up two by two to walk them down the road to school, which was only a few minutes away on St Patrick's Road.

I set off for home, stopping at the grocer's on the way to pick up some ingredients to make toffee apples, a special treat in the run-up to Bonfire Night. As I strolled back, clutching my bag of apples and sugar, my heart felt lighter than it had done in a long time. Julie had turned eighteen that year and seemed wonderfully happy after finally realising her ambition of joining the police force. She'd wanted to join the cadets when she was sixteen, but I had my reservations about her leaving home at such a young age. I had agreed that if she still wanted to join the police when she turned eighteen I wouldn't stand in her way. Even as she was filling in the application forms I tried to talk her out of it because I was afraid for her safety, and more than one person had told me that joining the force would change her. But she was determined. She passed all the tests and interviews with flying colours, as I knew she would, and they had written to tell her she'd been accepted. Davie and Chris were doing well in secondary school and I had recently spoken to their teachers, who told me that they were both top of their class that year. The twins had settled into their two different classes after being separated and were making new friends, always coming home and making me laugh with stories of what they'd been up to that day. Watching them play, confident and carefree, earlier that morning had made my problems with Kenny seem to fade away, and I walked slowly to enjoy the gentle warmth of the sun on my shoulders, knowing that it would likely be the last bright day we'd have until next spring. My bairns were happy so I was happy, and for the moment, all was well.

I busied myself setting out the ingredients for the toffee apples as soon as I was home, boiling up the water and sugar and watching it carefully as it turned into thick, dark caramel. The kitchen was filled with its sweet smell, and I was just skewering the apples and twirling them in the sauce when Kenny came in from his six-till-two shift. Without saying a word, he disappeared up to the bath, and I was distracted for a few moments as I went to take his work clothes from the cupboard for my next wash load. In the time that had taken, the warm toffee in the pan had cooled into a solid rock and I had to reheat it over and over as Kenny repeatedly summoned me upstairs to wash his back. After a few hours of this palaver, I finally managed to finish the last of the apples and set about cleaning up. The children came in from school, barrelling in one after another, squealing as they saw the lines of shiny red apples glinting on the counter.

It was beginning to grow dark by this time, and after the kids had had their tea and were smothered in sticky toffee, Kenny arrived downstairs dressed at last and announced that he was going to the seven o'clock evening Mass at St Anne's. It was nearly the twins' bedtime and I wanted to clean their teeth and put their pyjamas on – but they'd overheard their dad and with a little help from the sugar, were still energetic enough to want to go out again to church. How I wish I had stuck to my guns and not allowed myself to be swayed. More than anything else in my life, I wish I could turn the clock back and change that decision to let them go with him.

What happened next I can hardly bring myself to describe, it is so painful. Kenny told me he needed to call at the shops for tobacco after Mass, so I knew it would be well past eight o'clock when they all returned home. I was a little concerned about them going out, so I busied myself scrubbing the pots and pans in the kitchen with one eye on the clock, and then moved on to cleaning the living room. The whole house was sparkling by the time it turned eight, and I sat down and waited for the twins to come tumbling in again. But when it got to half-past eight I began to worry that something wasn't right. For a few minutes I waited outside the front door so I could see their little faces coming down the street, but then it became too cold and I came back in again, closing the door after me and shuddering as I rubbed my palms together briskly for warmth.

I was starting to feel anxious by now, but I kept telling myself I was being silly, they were with their father and they were probably just late because he'd taken his own sweet time buying his tobacco and stopping to light his pipe. I even wondered if he'd taken them for a shandy at the pub, the way he used to with Davie and Chris, but the twins would be falling asleep in their seats by now if he'd done that. At long last I heard a scrabble as the key turned in the door and I hurried out of the kitchen to see Kenny coming in, with Ian trailing behind. Alan was nowhere to be seen. My heart seemed to fall through my body at that moment. I immediately knew something terrible had happened and I flew at Kenny, screaming.

'Where is he?'

At first I couldn't take in Kenny's reply. He had to tell me twice before I could properly understand. Alan had been hit by a car on Fabian Road as they crossed to go to the shop.

My vision became blurred and Kenny's voice echoed towards me as though it was coming from the bottom of a well. I heard a loud whistling in my ears and I thought I was going to faint. I heard Ian crying and the floorboards creaking as the other two boys made their way downstairs. I looked at Ian, and back at Kenny again.

'Where is he now?' I asked, dreading the answer. 'What are you doing here without him? Why have you left him?'

Kenny lowered his head and muttered something. He hated hospitals, he was saying, so he couldn't go with him in the ambulance. I could only gaze at him in horror.

I shouted at Davie to run and bring Julie from her friend's house. He must have sprinted all the way there and back, because they were at our front door, breathless and pale, in no time. Julie told me she'd stopped at the scene of the accident on Fabian Road on her way over and asked the police where the ambulance had taken Alan, so she knew he was in Middlesbrough General Hospital, and she would drive me there. The image of Alan lying in the hospital all on his own was almost too much to bear and I begged Julie to overtake the cars that were lazily making their way home on what for them was an ordinary Thursday evening.

The journey to Middlesbrough normally took fifteen minutes, but that night it seemed to last for hours. Julie drove on and on, carefully turning left and right, gripping the steering wheel so tightly that her knuckles turned white. I didn't often pray – the last time I'd asked God for help was when I thought I was miscarrying the twins. Back then I was terrified for their lives but this was different. Alan was out there totally alone. In my head I began begging God or whoever was listening that Alan's injuries wouldn't be serious. I prayed to my mam, who we'd lost all those years ago before Julie was born, and begged her to protect my little boy. I prayed to my dad, who I knew would still want to keep his children and grandchildren from harm despite everything we'd gone through together. I prayed to Monna and Grandma and Grandad Burns.

Something strange happened after that. I began counting in my head. From one to a hundred, the same way Kenny did when he washed. When I reached a hundred, I would start back at the beginning. One, two, three, four... I told myself that as long as I kept counting, Alan would be all right. If I could count to a hundred enough times, perhaps I could wind the clock back to teatime, when Alan and Ian had been sitting at our kitchen counter, laughing at each other as they tried to free their teeth of toffee. One, two, three... Julie pulled into the car park. Seventeen, eighteen... We ran together across the tarmac and it was as though we were running through the thick toffee I had been stirring earlier, getting stiffer and stiffer as we tried to reach the hospital in time. Thirty-two, thirty-three... The bright lights of the hospital flickered distantly ahead, the space between us and the entrance stretching out like endless miles of deep black ocean. Fifty-nine, sixty.

By the time we reached the counter at the Accident and Emergency Department I was gasping for breath as I garbled out Alan's name to the nurse. My vision was still blurred and I felt I was seeing everything through one of those cardboard tubes the kids used when they were playing pirates. Everything at the peripheries was dark and shadowy, and at that moment all I could see was the nurse's face, bright under the harsh artificial hospital lights. I saw her expression change as she thumbed through the records in front of her and stopped at Alan's. I knew then that his condition was critical, without her needing to say a word. All of the hopes I had that I would see his smiling face waiting for me were sinking, but still I carried on counting. Ninety-nine, one hundred... My legs were like someone else's, beyond my control. I could feel my heart throbbing inside my chest and feared I was going to collapse before I even saw him.

The nurse took us into a small family room along the corridor and asked us to wait there. All the doctors and nurses were working on Alan, she said, but they would come and see us as soon as they could. Working on him? Just how bad was this? I started to pray again. 'Please God, don't let this be happening! Please don't let anything happen to my baby!' I sat bowed at the waist, my hands clasped together under my forehead. After counting more hundreds out in my mind I thought I was going to be sick, so I tried to stand to go to the toilet but found I couldn't. My body was shaking uncontrollably and I couldn't move my legs. I cried out to Julie, gasping in fear. She ran for help, and returned with a wheelchair for me as well as a nurse, who explained that it was the shock making my body react this way. Julie tried to reassure me everything would be all right. The doctors would take care of our Alan and make him better, she was certain of it. I managed to offer a token nod of agreement, but inside I was imagining the worst, and I never stopped counting, hearing Kenny's focused whispers in my head as I went round and round again.

The nurse left us and Julie and I sat together in that tiny green family room for what felt seemed to be an eternity. It was poorly lit and smelled of industrial cleaner that made us both feel faint and sick. We didn't say a word to one another, each of us worrying and praying and begging for Alan's life in our own way. I started counting in time with the clock on the wall, paying no notice to how many seconds passed. I must have reached tens of thousands by the time the doctors came to talk to us. They explained that Alan was still unconscious. It was the first time since Kenny had arrived back at the house all those hours ago that we heard the extent of my little boy's injuries. He had a fractured skull, a broken hip and severe bruising to his face. They said he was being looked after in intensive care. All I wanted to do was see him, and thankfully they agreed that we could go through at last.

Nothing could have prepared me for the sight of my poor baby. He looked so small and restful, as though he was just sleeping. Wires were strung out from his hands and chest and he was hooked up to all kinds of monitors. Four or five concerned-looking medical staff surrounded his bed, before they parted to allow us to be near him. His face and arms were covered in black and purple bruising, but the worst part of all was that I could tell he wasn't breathing normally. I kept praying and asking God to please help him. Still I counted, the rhythm matching my thudding heartbeat – I would count forever if it meant that my precious boy could wake up. But he didn't stir, and after only a few minutes together the nurses asked us to leave and we were escorted back to the family room again.

I don't know when they all arrived at the hospital but the room seemed to be full of people by the time we returned. I can't recall exactly who they were. I do remember Father Brennan coming in and asking where Kenny was. I tried to explain about Kenny's aversion to hospitals but Father Brennan didn't seem to take in what I was telling him and looked puzzled.

'I only just spoke to him on his way out of Mass and he seemed well enough,' he said. 'Surely he would want to be here with his son?'

How could he possibly understand? I had learned over the years not to bother trying to tell people about Kenny and what he would and wouldn't do. My own sisters had doubted me when I'd confided in them and I couldn't persuade the doctors to help, so what was the point of trying to explain it to anyone else if they weren't going to believe me anyway.

A policeman offered to go to collect Kenny and drive him over and Julie agreed to go with him and try to talk her father round. Whatever she said must have worked because later that night Kenny trudged in, still hanging his head as he had when he'd told me about the accident. I would have been shocked to see him set foot in a hospital if I hadn't been so dazed. He couldn't look at me which was fine because I paid him no attention as he sat down as far away from me as he could in the cramped family room, and I returned to my obsessive counting. Shortly afterwards a nurse arrived to take Kenny down to the room where our son was being cared for. He never returned. It was only later that I found out he'd taken one look at Alan lying there helpless in the bed and turned straight round again, walking out of the hospital and back down the road all the way home. As soon as he was inside the house he stripped naked and threw his clothes into the bin before climbing into the bath to scrub himself clean.

Meanwhile, the clock on the hospital wall ticked loudly and relentlessly. One by one the friends and relatives who had come to be with us left, and by one o'clock in the morning only Julie and I remained there together once more. She had been in and out of the room several times while I was rooted to my wheelchair and when she returned her eyes were bloodshot. I wondered if she knew more than she was telling me, and it turned out that she did. The consultant had taken her to one side and confided that Alan had suffered brain damage. The fracture was to the base of his skull, and his ear had cerebrospinal fluid coming from it. The doctor feared that Alan was unlikely to survive the night. Julie broke down, begging him to save her little brother.

'But you have all that equipment in there,' she pleaded. 'Please, you mustn't let him die.'

Later she told me she'd experienced the sensation of looking down on the scene from above, as though watching a video of the conversation taking place between two other people.

Deep in the early hours Julie and I were taken to another room with two beds in it. The nurse gently told us to try to get some sleep. But I just sat in the chair waiting and counting and staring. My heart and my head were pounding, and I didn't know what to do other than pray. I asked Our Lord – no, I begged him – not to take my child. I promised I would do anything if he would only spare the beautiful little boy who I had never asked for but he had given me. Julie fought to stay awake, getting up and moving around every few minutes, but eventually she grew so exhausted that she lay down with her head on my lap and finally fell into a restless sleep. I didn't feel entirely awake and drifted in and out of consciousness, counting and praying and losing my way and starting all over again. Ninety-nine, one hundred... Then I heard footsteps coming along the corridor and I was wide awake. But as soon as the nurse opened the door, I knew by the look on her face that my poor baby had gone. The endless numbers and all their futility evaporated in my head, along with all of my hopes and prayers. My darling Alan was dead.

'Please God, no!' I wailed. 'Don't let it be true!'

My cries roused Julie, and she woke to the dreadful news that her treasured baby brother had passed away. Even as I sobbed uncontrollably, barely able to catch my breath, I desperately needed to see him – I still couldn't believe or accept that he was gone – and the nurse agreed to take me. Julie stood up to follow, but I stopped her. I didn't want her lasting memory of her sweet little brother to be his lifeless body lying in a hospital bed. So I went alone, with just the nurse by my side as I said my goodbyes to my darling son. I have never felt such pain and devastation. I wanted to die myself and be with Alan again. No mother should ever have to see their child die before them, yet here I was gazing at the body of my own baby, who looked as though he was simply dreaming peacefully and would wake up at any moment.

I don't know how we arrived home but it was about five o'clock in the morning when we stumbled back through the front door. Kenny was slumped on the settee, half asleep, and he jumped to his feet as soon as we entered the room. I tried to say something, but my jaw remained clenched shut. I couldn't speak to him. I didn't even want to look at him. I went and stood in the cold kitchen, my arms tightly folded, emotionless. Julie was the one who had to tell Kenny what had happened. I heard a wild howl coming from the living room, a strangled noise unlike anything I'd ever heard before. Then came a loud thud and a scraping noise, as Kenny punched the wall and seemed to gouge at the wallpaper, as if to climb it. I took no notice. For once, our roles were reversed and it was me who said nothing and didn't react. As I turned away, I saw Alan's half-eaten toffee apple that I'd left on the side for when he came back from Mass, but for that moment I felt nothing. I was deep within a vast tidal wave of grief and had no thoughts at all.

I don't remember much about the week that led up to the funeral. Our house seemed to have an unceasing flow of family and friends calling in and expressing their sorrow and condolences. I sat chain-smoking, crying, and not knowing what to say or do. I didn't sleep. The sadness came in waves as I slipped in and out of a sort of hazy exhausted unconsciousness, reliving the horror over and over again as soon as I was aware enough to remember. I knew my life would never be the same again. I would never recover from the loss of my child. For a time, I believed that God was punishing me for my reaction of fear and even horror when I first fell pregnant with the twins. I truly wanted to die. Exiting this world seemed to be the only way my unbearable sorrow and agony could ever end.

On the day of the funeral, we followed my son in his little coffin into St Anne's Church. I saw Alan's classmates sitting together in two rows, singing the opening hymn. I kept thinking how only a few days earlier, on All Saints Day, Alan had sat with these same children. Now he was gone and they were still here. How could that be? How could life go on?

The service itself was a blur. I just know that I sobbed and wailed the whole time. I wouldn't let Ian come. This was no place for a child. He was too young to understand, and it would have been too harrowing and upsetting for him – he already had a lifetime of loss ahead of him. Instead, Margie had taken him to stay at her house for a few days. They carried Alan's coffin out of the church and I recall climbing unsteadily into the long black funeral car as we headed to Eston Cemetery for his burial. That's about all I can remember about the rest of that day, and the days that followed. I was like a zombie, neither living nor dead, asleep nor awake. My sisters started taking it in turns to come round to our house to help with the other kids and Julie was an angel, carrying on when I couldn't do anything for thinking of Alan. My sisters and friends tried to encourage me to focus on the other children, telling me how much they needed me, but it made no difference. I couldn't make my brain work as it once had. I was lost, and I didn't want to be found. My only wish was to disappear and never have to see anyone or do anything ever again. All of my boys needed me but I couldn't think straight or work anything out. I knew I had to get back on track and take care of my remaining family, but how? When I finally started sleeping again I would wake up in a grey cloud of depression and could barely find the strength to leave my bed. No-one knew what to do or what to say to me. After all, nothing would make me feel any better.

Alan's death hit Ian the hardest of all the children, as I expected it would. He was lost without his playmate and didn't know what to do with himself. It broke my heart all over again to see him so unhappy. Nothing any of us could do would ever make up for the death of his best friend, and having witnessed the horror unfold before his eyes must have made it even worse. I soon realised that he hated being on his own and couldn't bear to be without one of his friends with him. Fortunately, he was popular at school and his friends were there whenever he needed them.

I learned something amazing about children at that time – they are incredibly resilient. Ian and the others helped me to survive when I didn't think I could carry on because as they gradually got on with their lives, their example showed me that I could do it too. But it was going to take time. My panic attacks started one day when I was frying a pan of chips – a feeling of utter terror began to circulate in my stomach and then as it rose up I felt a sudden tightening in my chest, as though I was suffering a heart attack. I bent over in pain and could barely catch my breath. No-one was home at the time and I struggled desperately to inhale and exhale, as my stomach churned. The pain quickly passed, but I was left on the floor in frightened tears, as the chip pan bubbled away. Then the same thing happened when I was out at the shops, and again when I was walking the boys home from school, until finally my condition was so bad that Julie encouraged me to go to the doctor. He prescribed antidepressant tablets, warning me they can sometimes make people feel worse before they start to feel better. I didn't care, nothing could make me feel worse than I already did, so I popped the first pill with little more than a passing interest in the impact it might have on me. Maybe the pills numbed the pain a little, I don't know, but I continued to feel ill and deeply depressed. Life wasn't worth living. Words can't describe the loss of a child. My heart was torn in two and the pain in my chest was unremitting.

Kenny just sat in his armchair in a state of utter desolation: grieving, and in a deep depression. I didn't know what to say or do for him – I couldn't help myself, let alone anyone else. Whenever I came home or went into the lounge there he would be, in the same hunched position as when I'd left him. He kept trying to say he was sorry, telling me over and over that he couldn't do anything to stop the accident from happening, but I couldn't even look at him. Then he started following me around the house, pleading for forgiveness. But I didn't want to hear it. God and Father Brennan might forgive him but the absolution he wanted from me, I couldn't give.

'I'll never be able to escape my pain, and there's no escaping yours either,' I told him.

That's the burden and the responsibility of being a parent, you take the joy and you take the pain. I wanted him to just leave me alone, but he wouldn't. Then one day, weeping bitterly, he grabbed hold of my wrists.

'You have to forgive me, Joanie!'

I told him to leave me alone, but he clung on, sobbing. And so eventually, to my everlasting shame, I took off a slipper and struck his body hard with it, until he finally did let go.

After that I only spoke to Kenny when it was strictly necessary. After all, what was there to say? Neither of us could alter anything. Our lives were changed forever. Nothing would ever bring Alan back.

17

THE NUMB YEARS

J ulie had been working at the police headquarters in Middlesbrough for a few weeks before the terrible accident. The week after Alan's funeral, an inspector came to the house and announced that they wanted her to start her ten-week initial training course in Dishforth. I had been relying on her so much that her first reaction was to tell them she couldn't go because she didn't want to leave me the way I was. But I insisted that she did. I wanted her to follow her dreams and couldn't stand in her way. So a few days later, she set off for the police training school in Dishforth. I missed her every day and looked forward to her weekly visits home.

I don't know how long it was before I returned to work but my little job at St Mary's eventually helped save my sanity and kept me going, along with the support of family and friends. I certainly didn't go back for the money. I earned £15 a week, but because Kenny was on the sick now I was only £5 a week better off than if I'd stayed at home. Some people thought I was crazy, but I didn't care. It made me feel that I was contributing to the world in some small way and got me out of the house, which had once been filled with laughter but had turned into a pit of gloom, with Kenny sitting in his armchair day after day, doing nothing and speaking to nobody.

Kenny never went back to work after Alan's death. He was still on the sick when he was offered redundancy from British Steel early the following year and he took it without even mentioning it to me. Not that I cared. He was unfit for any type of work – that much had been clear for a long time – but as usual, he wouldn't see a doctor. He had never offered me much in the way of emotional support, but by now he was too ill to change even if he'd wanted to, and he simply sat at home for hours on end without moving a muscle. We'd never had a joint bank account and all of Kenny's redundancy money went into his personal account, but by this point he was in such a bad way that he couldn't so much as leave the house to draw out the money I needed to feed us all. He wouldn't let me do it for him, either, because only he was allowed to touch it. In desperation, I found his chequebook and wrote out a cheque for £20, which I cashed at the Yorkshire Bank in Eston. Kenny was furious and reported me to the bank manager.

Watching Ian grow up left me always wondering what Alan would have looked and sounded and smelled like. I blamed myself ceaselessly for leaving him in Kenny's care, and hated having to spend my days with someone I believed had neglected his duties as a parent and failed to prevent an avoidable accident. That may sound harsh, but I had asked Kenny so many times to keep a closer eye on the twins. He never took any notice of me. He just told me I worried too much, that they weren't babies any more and they needed their freedom. Call it mother's intuition, but I always had a feeling of dread that something terrible might happen to them.

Although the pain in my heart never went away, as the months went by I somehow learned to lock it away and try to get on with my life. I don't know what I would have done without Julie. The night before her first day on patrol as a police officer, my words of advice to her were to always treat people the way she would wish to be treated herself. She promised me she would, and I know that's exactly what she did.

When she came back home after her training, she started giving me £25 a week lodge money, which seemed a fortune – Kenny's sickness benefit was only £30 a week. Thanks to Julie's contribution and my wages from St Mary's, it was an intense relief to know that at last I would no longer have to be constantly fretting about money.

But while I was clawing my way out of my own depression, Kenny plunged helplessly deeper and deeper into his. He still wouldn't leave the house, and hardly moved from his chair for days, but he still refused to go to the doctor. The responsibility for lifting him out of his grief seemed to fall at my feet, but I was in no fit state to help him. Finally, after many months, the GP came to our house, just as he had all those years before, except this time Kenny couldn't run away. The doctor prescribed antidepressants, but he told me Kenny's mental health was in such a poor state that he really needed to be in St Luke's psychiatric hospital. He was seriously concerned that Kenny might harm himself, but he emphasised that it had to be Kenny's decision and, of course, nobody could persuade him to go. I didn't know what to do, or who to turn to. Just as I was beginning to win the daily battle I fought with my own feelings of hurt and anger, now I had to worry about Kenny as well.

And then the night before Alan's first anniversary, Kenny somehow managed to get hold of a bottle of vodka and some painkillers – I've no idea where from. He waited until everyone else had gone to bed before he swallowed the lot, together with his antidepressants. I still don't know to this day what made me decide to check on him, but I awoke in the early hours and went downstairs to find Kenny slumped on the living room sofa, ice-cold and unconscious. I thought he was dead. I ran up to Julie's room, crying and babbling incoherently. When she finally understood what I was saying, she ran down and phoned for an ambulance. Then she laid him on the floor and put her police training to use by carrying out chest compressions on her dad until help arrived. Exactly a year after Alan's death we found ourselves in Middlesbrough General Hospital once again, in the exact same ward with the exact same staff. Repeating our steps through those dreadful, familiar corridors ripped open old wounds, and I relived that terrible night all over again.

Kenny was unconscious for two whole days before he finally started to come round. The doctors told him he needed to be admitted to St Luke's, but once again he flatly refused and he discharged himself shortly afterwards. As soon as he was home, he hurried straight off to the bath and refused to come out until after midnight. When he did emerge from the bathroom I couldn't believe what he had done to himself. All of his old sores on his knees and elbows and his hands had been opened back up, and new raw patches had appeared where the upper layers of skin had been sluiced clean off into the bathwater. The towel was stained with bloody marks, and his body was covered in great cross-hatched areas of angry red where he'd used the flannel to tear away at his skin. Even after he was dressed, the bright marks were clearly visible below his sleeves and above his collar.

Julie had had enough, and decided to literally take the law into her own hands. She put on her police uniform and told him that if he didn't go with her to the hospital, she would have to arrest him. Kenny didn't have the energy left to fight, and at long last, after years of tears and arguments and frustration, my daughter managed to take him to St Luke's as a voluntary inpatient. Each time I visited, he would tell me he didn't need to be there. He wasn't like the other patients, he said, and he begged me to let him come home. Well, he soon got his wish. The doctors said they couldn't do anything more to help him because he wouldn't cooperate with them in any way, and so he was discharged.

That's probably the most difficult part of living with someone with a condition such as Kenny's. It's not their fault that they are trapped inside their own mind, a slave to the obsessive, negative thoughts that their brain subjects them to. Nor is it their fault that compulsive behaviours follow, which they are forced to act out over and over again to try to cleanse their mind of the unwanted urge. It also wasn't Kenny's fault that he was born at a time when people understood so little about OCD and the many other mental illnesses that afflicted our generation, nor that he'd experienced trauma and neglect as a child. But here's what was his fault – he never, ever admitted that he had a problem, as a starting point for seeking help. The years of destruction – missed births, a miserable marriage, a home life under constant strain, and perhaps even the death of his own son – were all a consequence of Kenny's stubborn insistence that he didn't need help, because I was imagining everything. People who are living with a mental illness must seek help for themselves. Not for their friends, not for their wife, not for their children, but for themselves. Until that happens, nothing you say or do will have an impact. I thought about how, all those years ago when I was pregnant with Chris, I'd packed up our tiny house to force Kenny's hand. He didn't move for me or the kids, but because it was preferable to the only alternative of staying put with nothing. For his own sake, he needed to learn how to confront his illness instead of using me and our home as a screen to conceal it, but I couldn't see that happening in our future.

Poor Kenny was at his wits' end. He continued to feel distraught and unable to live with what had happened. He was so desperate that he attempted suicide twice more. The first time, Julie found him. The second time it was Chris. But still he refused all offers of help.

I firmly believe it was a dog that saved Kenny's life in the end. We'd never kept pets (apart from Chris's ill-fated hamster) but Julie brought home a 'Heinz 57-variety' black puppy and persuaded us to let her keep it. She'd thought it was a male, but it turned out to be a bitch, and our kids decided to call her 'Lassie'. Kenny and Lassie became the best of friends, and the dog helped him immeasurably. Walking Lassie was the one thing that motivated Kenny to leave the house again and encouraged him to enjoy life on his own terms, rather than being governed by his compulsions. I had never wanted a dog before, but I was eternally grateful that Lassie came into our lives when she did.

We never had a shortage of volunteers to take the dog out for walks. One morning, we found her lying in her basket in the kitchen with her legs shaking, so I asked Julie to take her to the vets for a check-up. When they arrived back a couple of hours later Julie had a right face on. The vet had told her Lassie was perfectly healthy, it was just that the kids had over-walked the poor little bugger and worn her out!

When Julie showed me her first payslip after she graduated from training school I was speechless. £300! I couldn't believe it. She was sensible with her money and when she confided to a colleague that she had some savings, he suggested that rather than buying a new car she should invest in property, as it would increase in value. So she took heed and bought a little bungalow in Eston. I was dejected to see her go, but at the same time my heart swelled with pride to see her finding her wings.

We were having our tea one evening, not long after she'd left home, when I heard a sharp knock on the door. I opened it to see a young policeman standing there and I invited him in, thinking he must be looking for Julie. But to my astonishment, he had come to tell me that they had received a report about me from one of my neighbours. It emerged that Penny next door had told them I'd murdered a baby in Cornwall many years ago, and she claimed to have two witnesses – Elizabeth Taylor and John Hurt! I'd never been to Cornwall in my life and the police realised it was nonsense, but I was upset and shaken. I already knew that poor Penny's mental health wasn't good. A few months earlier, she'd pushed a letter through our door telling me she wanted the car back that I'd stolen from her. I had no idea what she was talking about – we didn't even have a car.

By this time, we had a social worker assigned to us, and she and I had a startlingly frank conversation one day while Kenny was out walking Lassie. Looking at me over her teacup, and without mincing her words, she told me that I should leave him. She was convinced that he would never change, he was too self-centred and wrapped up in his own problems, and she was afraid that he would drag me back down with him. I'd often thought of leaving Kenny before but now I just couldn't bring myself to do it, I felt too sorry for him. I certainly didn't love him any more – Kenny had killed our love slowly but surely with his selfishness over the years – but I somehow felt responsible for him and I couldn't be so cruel as to leave him all alone after everything that had happened.

So the years dragged on, and if it was the dog that saved Kenny's life, then it was my boys who saved mine. They still needed me, and they pulled me through that hard, sad, depressing time in my life. In 1985 we moved to Woodlands Close in the nearby Bankfields estate. I was reluctant to leave behind our family home in Deepdale Avenue with all the memories it held, but I hoped circumstances might improve if we made a fresh start. Unfortunately, our situation didn't get any better over there and I hated the new house, which I found cramped and badly designed. I tried to make the best of it for Davie, Chris and Ian, but I never really settled there.

Our lads were lovely. They were growing up fast and doing well at school. I was so proud of Davie when he managed to get an apprenticeship as a shipbuilding draughtsman at Smith's Dock. For me this meant he would be a skilled worker, able to find a good job with a decent wage. When he wanted to marry and start a family, he would be in a position to properly support them.

Eighteen months later, Chris also left school. He was every bit as clever as Davie but he was nervous in his interviews, and just missed out on an apprenticeship at ICI Wilton. Instead, he ended up on the dole the same as Kenny, something I had dreaded – I wanted better for my sons. Chris was becoming more and more like his father in both looks and temperament as he grew into a young man. He didn't yet have much self-confidence or ambition to better himself, but I didn't want him to end up the same as us, in a rented house with no money or prospects. I told him that no-one was going to come knocking at our door offering him work, and that he needed to go out and find a job that he really wanted to do. This caused further arguments with Kenny, who accused me of making Chris's life a misery. When it became clear that there just weren't any jobs to be had, I encouraged Chris to enrol on a mechanical maintenance course at Longlands College in Middlesbrough. It was the best thing he could have done. I was thrilled for him and full of pride when he went on to join the RAF, training in radio and telephone communications and earning an excellent wage.

After Smith's Dock closed down in 1987, Davie got a job in a drawing office at Tynemouth. It was over an hour's journey there and back, which was tough after an eight-hour day. He had been courting a sweet girl called Andrea for a while, and their engagement was the first happy event in our family since we'd lost Alan. They organised a party upstairs in the Normanby pub and invited all our family and friends. We ate a delicious meal together and both mothers were given beautiful bouquets of flowers. As Davie and Andrea posed for photographs, I blinked away tears of joy at the thought of all the happiness their future lives would bring them. Later, I watched on in amazement as the young ones danced to *Oops Upside Your Head* (a chart hit at the time) while they sat on the floor – how different from the type of dancing I used to do at the local church halls in my teens! The room was filled with laughter, and we celebrated late into the night.

Davie and Andrea arranged their wedding for May 1987. They booked St Gregory's Catholic Church on Bankfields Road for the ceremony, and the reception was to take place at the Marton Country Club, a smart venue that was popular for weddings. But when Kenny found out where the reception was going to be, he refused point-blank to attend. His aversion to anything medical was so extreme that he couldn't bear the idea of going to the country club because he thought it was too close to the hospital. He said he would go to the church, but not the reception.

We tried our best to persuade him and Julie even offered to take him along the A174 in her car so he could see that the hotel was several miles away from the hospital, but to no avail. He just refused to listen and would walk away whenever the subject was raised. I was distraught. I was used to him showing me up, but I couldn't bear the thought of him ruining Davie's special day. Finally, in desperation, the sweet-talking turned to threats.

'If you do this to me and our Davie, I'll never speak to you again,' I warned him.

Before we knew it, the wedding day was upon us. I was a nervous wreck in the morning, hoping and praying that Kenny would behave himself and not embarrass us. I must have been kidding myself. As soon as the ceremony was over, he somehow managed to sneak away from the church without anyone seeing him. Nobody knew where he had gone. Devastated and humiliated, I arrived at the hotel and sat down at the top table, with an empty seat beside me where the groom's father should have been. People kept asking me where he was. Others were tactful enough not to mention his absence – but even those who knew him were at a loss to understand how he could miss such an occasion. The truth is, there simply was no fathoming Kenny McGowan.

A couple of years later, Ian left school and started working as a trainee chef at Redcar Golf Club. He loved the job but hated the long hours and the poor pay, and he started looking around for an apprenticeship or some other type of training. At the time there was nothing on offer, but when he started talking about joining the RAF as Chris had, I was beside myself. Ian was the last of the kids still at home. Kenny and I already slept in separate rooms and led virtually separate lives, and I just couldn't face the prospect of being left alone with him.

Then early one morning Julie phoned to say she felt unwell with severe stomach pains. She had always suffered from painful periods and had been brought home from work several times because of it, but she said this felt worse. I'd had my appendix removed when I was seventeen and Davie had his taken out when he was only twelve, and the way Julie described the pain sounded worryingly similar. I ran round to her house so quickly that she joked I must have flown there on my broomstick! At least she still had her sense of humour, even though it was obvious she was in great pain. The doctor arrived shortly afterwards and confirmed appendicitis. Julie was taken to Middlesbrough General by ambulance and a few hours later her appendix was removed. I visited her there the next day, and she told me she would only be allowed home if she had someone there to look after her. Naturally, I said I'd do it, and I went to stay at her house with her when she was discharged.

Being there felt like being released from a long, miserable prison sentence, with the added bonus of being able to look after my daughter again. I'd never anticipated how relieved I would feel to be away from Kenny. We'd been stuck together leading sad, unfulfilled lives for so many years, and in all that time I'd had no hope or means of ever leaving. The first night I slept at Julie's it felt as though all that had changed.

After a few weeks Julie started to feel well enough to cope on her own, and that was when I realised I just couldn't go back to Kenny. I couldn't bear the idea of returning once I'd experienced the light of freedom after half a lifetime of living in the dark. I was already in my late forties, and my children were all grown up and leading their own lives. I didn't even like Kenny, let alone love him. I had given him my best years, and for what? Row after row, weeks spent in total silence, and a bathtub filled with tears!

Now I was out, and I didn't intend to waste another day with him. It was only a matter of weeks before Ian would be joining the RAF, and I knew this might be my only chance to escape. If I'd gone back to live in that gloomy house alone with Kenny, destined to be his servant until the end of our days, I think it would have killed me.

18

LEARNING TO BREATHE AGAIN

We talked it over with a bottle of wine one night, and Julie agreed to help me. She knew how unhappy I was. After all, she'd lived through the dark days alongside me. She knew all about the difficulties of living with her father, and how I had striven to accommodate his unreasonable demands. I couldn't face going back to the house to collect my belongings. I was frightened that if I did, I would give in to Kenny's pleas for me to stay. So Julie went instead, returning with two bin liners containing all my clothes and a couple of photo albums. I was leaving him, not the other way round, and I didn't want anything else. After that, I spoke to our boys and explained how I felt. They understood – they all knew exactly what Kenny was like. Even so, although I implored him to come with me, Ian wouldn't leave his father, and I admired him for that.

With Julie's help I started looking for a new place to live. I wasn't eligible for a council house, but eventually we managed to find a one-bedroomed flat above Heagney's shop on the corner of Normanby High Street. It was small and poky but it was mine, and I had my freedom at long last. It was the summer of 1988 and at nearly fifty years of age I was living on my own for the first time in my life. I can't say I was happy. I was relieved to have escaped from Kenny but I was also worried, and afraid of what the future might hold for me. I had never had to fend for myself before, my sisters and friends all had their own families and concerns – I was lost. For all my experience of caring for fragile babies, boisterous toddlers and older kids, when I was on my own I didn't know which way to turn or what to do next.

Lonely as I was, the company that came my way was not exactly what I had in mind. The flat became infested with mice, attracted by rubbish left behind the shop. I only spotted one to start with. It was sitting motionless beside the skirting board, and at first I thought it was a large brown balled-up sock that had escaped the washing basket, but when I turned back round it had disappeared. Then later I opened the door to see a ball of fluff dart from one side of the hallway to the other, leaving behind the trail of crumbs it had been munching on. After that, more of them came. The last straw was when I woke up one night to see a mouse sitting on the edge of my bed looking straight at me! I screamed blue murder and the little devil ran away, but I wasn't hanging around to see if it would be back with the rest of its family. I packed an overnight bag and headed over to Julie's, where I stayed until we managed to rid the flat of my unwelcome guests.

Although my new beginning was stressful, as is so often the case in life, the pieces just gradually fell into place. As I grew braver, I managed to find a job as a care assistant at an old people's home, Eston House. At first I was nervous and unsure of myself, but I soon grew to love it. The shifts were tiring and when I was in the flat I was usually too exhausted to do anything but clean up and sleep. But I was no stranger to hard work or the care and compassion that the job required, and I loved the fact that I was supporting myself by looking after other people – which felt genuinely worthwhile. I've always been soft-hearted, and I felt a great deal of sympathy for the old folk who lived there. Some of them never seemed to have a single visitor, even though I knew they had families. It was heartbreaking that their children seemed to have forgotten about them and couldn't even spare an hour or two of their time now and then. I dedicated myself to making sure their days were filled with lively conversation and some kindness and laughter, to try to ease the pain their children's absence no doubt caused.

I didn't enjoy every aspect of the work, but when I found myself hesitating to respond to the assistance bell, I told myself it could have been my mam or dad. Then it was easy to wash and take care of the residents' personal needs, and even to dodge the odd punch or slap from an old dear who was confused and starting down the road towards dementia. I never minded listening to the same stories over and over again, no matter how pointless or illogical they seemed to be, because I knew those stories were their most cherished memories – even if the images became hazier and hazier until they were eventually just strung-together snapshots of the people and places they'd once known. It broke my heart to see someone suffering from dementia return for just a moment, the light filling their eyes in a brief few seconds of recognition, before fading away again, lost in the fog. When that happened I had to hide my face while I brushed away a tear or two, thinking about my own grandparents and my mother. Mind you, I wasn't a completely soft touch. I lost my temper with some of the younger girls working there who seemed to take their own sweet time to respond to the bell. I reminded them that, sure enough, one day they would be old and frail, and would need assistance just as our residents did. How would they feel if they were made to wait to use the loo?

Little by little, I grew to appreciate my independence. I found that I enjoyed going out with friends again. Sometimes as I was getting ready, I'd cast my mind back to those early days when I felt my life was just beginning – remembering how I'd pick out my clothes in the little back bedroom of our house in North Ormesby and ask Margie to set my hair with sugar water. Mam, leaning tiredly against the door frame, would check me over before I left the house to make sure I didn't have a ladder in my tights or a loose hem on my skirt, and she'd make me do a twirl for her.

'You take after your mother,' she'd say proudly, then she'd remind me of her terms – no drinking, no going over the border, and be back home by ten o'clock, non-negotiable! But now I had no-one to tell me what was out of bounds any more, no mother or husband to set the rules, and in some ways that frightened me. Freedom comes with a price tag, and I'd lost some of the sense of security and belonging I'd held onto my whole life.

My bathroom was fitted with a shower, the first one I'd ever had, and I enjoyed the feeling of raindrops lightly running over my face. After everything I'd experienced, I never wanted another bath ever again, but I finally learned to enjoy taking care of myself. When I gazed at my reflection in the mirror, I saw the changes the years had brought. My face had aged of course, but my hair was still the same fair shade it had always been, with only one or two silver threads running through it. I no longer had the skinny frame of a teenager – I had given birth to five children and my body now bore scars and traces of the full but difficult life I'd lived. But the biggest difference was in my head. Unlike the happy-go-lucky young lass I once was, I now had psychological wounds, deep lines of scar tissue that rippled across my memories. They had been too painful to touch, reopening at the slightest thought of Alan. But over time they were gradually healing, becoming paler like those on my skin. They would always be there, but they didn't ache as bitterly any more.

The final step on my journey was difficult. Kenny and I had been separated for months now but I was still wearing my gold wedding band out of habit, even though I had to take it off for my shifts at the care home. I removed it now for the last time, observing the thin band of lighter skin it left behind, permanently indented into the base of my finger after so many years of wear. It felt strange and sad, but the ring had been a residual reminder of Kenny and my responsibility to him, and I was ready to let it go at last. I put it inside my old wooden jewellery box, and tucked the box underneath the layers of folded clothes in my chest of drawers. Safely locked away, along with so many other memories buried in my heart.

I was proud that I'd managed to start again from scratch, with nothing but the bin bags of belongings that Julie had rescued for me. But my new life was lonely at times. I longed for love and companionship, and the warmth that Kenny was never able to give me. My children were all grown up, and didn't seem to need me as they used to. Then one day at the care home I started chatting to a man who had come in to do some maintenance work. We hit it off, and to my surprise he asked me out. We began seeing each other regularly, but it wasn't long before I sensed that I'd jumped out of the frying pan and into the fire. He turned out to be threatening and controlling, and it took me some time to extricate myself from the relationship and win back my freedom.

In the meantime, the council had written to offer me a ground-floor flat back in Eston, and I wasted no time moving in. It was small, but far more comfortable than my old place. The lounge had a large picture window, and the flat was warm and cosy, with central heating – sheer luxury – and best of all, no mice! I threw myself into decorating my new home and soon had it looking just how I wanted it.

I felt happy and settled there in no time, and then I received a wonderful piece of news that brought a new and fulfilling role to my life. Julie was pregnant. I was going to be a grandmother!

19

A SECOND CHANCE

Many years had passed since I'd seen or heard from my first love, Byron. I had popped round to Margie's for a cup of tea one afternoon when she told me she'd overheard a conversation on another table at her Women's Institute meeting. Somebody had mentioned the name 'Byron' – not one you hear every day – and Margie wondered if they were talking about my old boyfriend. She learned that they were, and that his wife Jean had sadly passed away. Margie remembered Byron fondly from our youth, just as I did, and she persuaded me to get in touch with him. We'd lost contact long ago but fortunately his address was listed in the phone book, so I wrote him a little 'Thinking of you' card. I just wanted to tell him how genuinely sorry I was about what had happened and to let him know that I was here if he needed a shoulder to cry on. Although I didn't know the pain of losing a beloved partner, I too had suffered a terrible loss in my life and I had some idea of how he might be feeling.

A couple of days later the phone rang. I answered, expecting it to be Julie calling for a chat and was taken aback to hear Byron's voice instead. The tone was richer and deeper now, but he was still unmistakably the boy I had met in the school playground and fallen in love with when I was just a girl. The last time we'd spoken was in the street in South Bank, not long after we had each married someone else. But in some ways it felt as though we had never been apart, and we spent the best part of an hour reminiscing and filling each other in on some of what had happened since our lives had taken such different paths. At the end of the call we arranged to meet the following Saturday evening. I felt a flutter in my stomach I had not experienced for many, many years as I replaced the receiver, and I thought about little else but Byron in the days that followed.

By the time Saturday came around I felt fourteen again. I sat waiting for him to pick me up, dressed in my best clothes with my hair pinned up neatly, counting down the minutes as unwanted thoughts gatecrashed my happiness. Would he still be angry with me for breaking up with him the way I did? What if he didn't like me any more? And then came the moment I feared would never arrive, as Byron's car finally pulled up outside my little flat. After a last glance in the mirror, I opened the front door and stepped outside to greet him. We didn't say a single word to each other. I just took one look at the expression on his face and we fell into each other's arms and for a few minutes we stayed that way, locked in the comfort of an embrace that said more than words ever could. As I held onto him, a great weight lifted off my shoulders and I felt that I was coming home after a long lifetime away.

Byron drove us to the Half Moon pub in Lazenby, a country village in the shadow of the huge steelworks and ICI chemicals complexes that used to dominate Teesside, and we sat and talked over a couple of quiet drinks, laughing as we recalled old times, and becoming hushed and serious as we delved more deeply into what had happened to us both in the years we'd been apart. To me it was all a miracle. The man sitting in front of me was older and greyer than the boy I'd known, but I was united once more with my best friend, my soulmate. It felt startling and exciting, with a sense of magic in the air between us. I dared to hope that it might just be possible to find happiness again – something that had seemed unthinkable only a few months earlier.

Byron told me about poor Jean's illness. She had had two malignant melanomas removed from her leg and had gone into hospital for further treatment, but she never came back home again. I could feel his pain as he poured his heart out to me, brimming with emotion. Then he told me something that Jean had said to him not long before she died. They were alone together, and she had taken his hand and held it tightly.

'I have something to say,' she said. 'I know I don't have long left, but please be happy when I'm gone. A lovely lady is waiting for you and has been waiting for many, many years. Make her as happy as you have made me.'

Jean was in a bad way by this time and Byron thought it was the morphine making her say such strange things. Now, in the dim light of the pub, his face was earnest.

'I honestly believe she knew I would meet you again,' he said, his eyes glistening with tears.

I couldn't stop myself from crying too. It was tragic that Byron had lost Jean after so many happy years together, but I was so grateful that she had given us her blessing to be friends again.

After that evening, our relationship took off. We were older, wiser, and much more aware of how fleeting and precious life is. It passes in the blink of an eye and you never know what's round the corner, or how quickly everything can change. We had both suffered unbearable losses and we wanted to try to find some comfort and a little happiness in the years we had left, with the support of a loving partner by our side.

Byron looked so painfully thin and lost that I couldn't help but take him to my heart. He wasn't used to cooking and looking after himself. Later, when I met his brother and sister-in-law, Dennis and Eileen, they told me how worried they were about him. They said he seemed to have been wasting away since Jean's death. I was introduced to Byron's son Keith and the rest of his family during a short break we enjoyed at Centre Parcs in the Lakes. We all had such a wonderful time there that Byron and I soon booked another trip together for just the two of us, to Majorca. I couldn't believe how easily our relationship was developing, although we were taking it slowly because we so appreciated being together again at last.

We set off for Spain like a pair of young lovers. But while we were there, our bliss was shattered when Byron became unwell and we had to call a doctor. We couldn't speak Spanish and the doctor spoke only broken English, so I couldn't really understand what he was telling us. Byron ended up being ill in bed for eight days, and I became increasingly worried about him. I felt so far from home and my children, and terrified that I was going to lose him so soon after finding him once more.

Thank God, he made a full recovery. We didn't see much of the sunshine on that holiday, but we made up for it by spending our time together talking. I showed Byron how much I loved him by taking care of him and he appreciated my efforts in a way that I'd never experienced before. Where Kenny had believed it was simply my duty as a wife, Byron knew that I looked after him because I wanted to, not because I had to, and he was happy and grateful for that. We were both reminded of how fragile life is. When we came back from Majorca our relationship was stronger than ever.

Byron and I occasionally stayed together – we were grown-up after all – and then in March 1995 he asked me to move in with him. I felt elated and excited, although I was also more than a little apprehensive. At first I was racked with guilt and could still sense Jean's presence in the house. But Byron made me feel that I was myself again. Sometimes late at night I would come alive, and couldn't resist bursting into song and dancing round the room before getting washed and ready for bed. You'd think I was seventeen again! Maybe Mam was right about me missing my calling – I should have had a career on the stage because I always did love to entertain, and make people laugh.

Every night without fail before we went to sleep I would tell Byron how much I loved him, how special he made me feel, and how grateful I was for all his love and kindness. He would say the same, then we'd kiss goodnight, I'd say my prayers, read my book for a little while, and drift contentedly off to sleep. Looking back now, I have to pinch myself when I think how much my life changed after I met Byron again. If only we hadn't broken up in the first place! But no – I wouldn't have it any other way. I love my children so much, and if I had made different choices I wouldn't have them, so how could I want to change anything?

It's such as shame that some people can't bear to see others happy. Tongues wagged, and a few unkind comments were made about us to our families. Julie was upset when a work colleague tried to tell her that Byron and I had been seeing each other while poor Jean was dying in hospital. Julie and I have always been close and she knew me better than anyone else in the world. She was affronted because she knew for a fact that it wasn't true. But I had no time for gossip – Julie had recently given birth to my first grandchild, Eleanor Jane (named after my mam), and I was far too busy relishing being a grandmother! I adored spending time with the family, and being able to help out by babysitting, and I was so proud to see that all my children were successfully making their own way in life.

In 1997, Byron asked me to marry him. It just seemed to be the natural next step for both of us – we were meant to be together. Later that year, Byron and I drove south with Dennis and Eileen, took the overnight ferry to Jersey, and enjoyed a wonderful fortnight at the Sunshine Hotel in St Helier. It was a holiday I'll never forget.

I'd wanted to visit the Jersey Tunnel Exhibition, which tells the story of the German occupation during World War II, because I had read about it and was interested to learn more. But as soon as we walked through the entrance I stopped dead, rooted to the spot. I instinctively felt that something evil had happened there and I turned as cold as ice and started shivering, even though the day was warm. In the end, only Byron and Dennis went in, as I just couldn't bring myself to go any further. Intuitions like this were something I'd started to experience more and more. I often felt that my mother and old Monna were with me, every now and then feeling the warmth of a hand on my shoulder – only to turn around and realise nobody was there. Rarely, just once or twice, I even thought I could hear the delightful sound of Ian and Alan's laughter, as though they were playing upstairs together just as they used to. Perhaps it was a gift that I'd always had, but never had the energy to tap into until my life finally settled down.

On the last day of the holiday in St Helier, Byron took me to a jeweller and asked me to choose a ring so we could become formally engaged. That night, we all went to a wonderful restaurant to celebrate, and I couldn't stop admiring the glittering diamonds in my ring, scattering tiny rainbows around the room in the candlelight.

We were married at Guisborough Registry Office on June 6th, 1998. I asked Margie to be my best woman – it just felt right that my closest sister should be by my side as I married the man I loved, just as she had always been there for me throughout my life, with all its highs and lows. I wore a pale turquoise outfit and carried a small bouquet of forget-me-nots and lily of the valley. Shortly before I left the house I felt another disturbing premonition – I was terrified that someone would step forward as I walked into the room and snatch my bouquet from me. I was shaking so much that the beautiful petals began to fall out, covering my outfit in tiny white and lilac dots. But it turned out to be nothing but pre-wedding nerves – the day was perfect in every way. The sun beamed down, and all my family and friends were there for our reception at the magnificent Guisborough Hall, with its stunning views of the Cleveland Hills. Everyone looked thrilled for us both, and Byron and I were overjoyed.

Afterwards, we returned to beautiful St Helier for our honeymoon. On the first full day there we woke up to the sound of heavy rain on the windows and a force eight gale blowing outside, but we still went out in the car and had lunch at our favourite restaurant overlooking the bay, while we watched the Oriana cruise ship being tossed about on the sea. As we left the restaurant I suggested a walk on the beach, despite the awful weather. Byron must have thought I was mad, but being the perfect gentleman, he agreed. When we arrived there I was so exhilarated that I started running along the sand, belting out *Singing in the Rain* at the top of my voice! I was a teenager again. Byron was still laughing gently as he drove us back to our hotel.

'Only you would do that, Joanie,' he said affectionately.

I smiled back at him, then gazed silently out of the car window. The storm was clearing, making way for an enormous double rainbow arching across the sky above us. I looked down at my wedding ring.

'Promise me you won't ever give me any reason to take this ring off,' I said.

But I knew with all my heart that he never would.

And what about Kenny? Well, he ended up meeting Kathleen at a local tea dance (ironic isn't it, when you think of how he would never come dancing with me?). Men were in short supply at the dance, and I heard that a few of the older ladies were fighting over him but Kathleen won the day, and in time the two of them became an item. He even asked her to marry him, but she declined. Having lost her husband of many years, she was content to just be good friends – and they went on holiday together, the boys told me. But I must confess I barely gave them a moment's thought. I felt so lucky to have my second chance with Byron.

He was always so kind and thoughtful. We loved going away together, and made a host of happy memories. We visited Italy one year and stayed in a small village just off the shores of Lake Ledro. During the second week I became quite upset. I'd always had problems with my hearing, ever since the swimming pool accident when I was a child. At mealtimes we shared our table with two other couples and spent our evenings in the same company, but I was struggling to keep up with the conversation. I felt left out and worried that the others might think I was being rude. As usual, Byron was my knight in shining armour. He told me not to worry, that everything was fine and once we arrived home he would make arrangements to find a solution for me. True to his word, he made me a private appointment and I was fitted with digital hearing aids, which cost thousands of pounds. Byron said it was the best money he had ever spent and that I was worth every penny. I had never been made to feel so special in my life.

We both loved Italy and visited twice more after that first time, spending many happy hours being rowed along the canals of Venice and exploring the churches of Florence, Padua and Verona – not bad for a woman who'd turned fifty without ever leaving the confines of Middlesbrough! I have to smile when I remember a coach trip we took to southern France with Eileen and Dennis. The driver stopped for a break and I was desperate for the loo, but I'd never seen anything as basic as the facilities on offer – it was nothing more than a hole in the ground! Desperate as I was, I just couldn't go, much to the amusement of the others. What a relief it was when we eventually found a proper toilet!

Going abroad was wonderful, but because of my ear problems flying was painful, so Byron would always be looking for somewhere new and interesting to take me to in this country. We visited Bath, Chester and the Lake District, among many other lovely places in England. No matter where we went, our priority was always to make each other happy and enjoy ourselves, and we invariably have. He's taken me to the Peak District, and the Isle of Wight, where we spent hours looking around Osborne House and marvelling at the architecture of the quaint old churches. I love visiting ancient cathedrals and estates such as Chatsworth House, and Byron has made it all possible. On one trip I took a liking to a delicate china coffee cup with a matching saucer, and without a moment's hesitation he was at the counter buying it for me. Now wherever we go he'll buy me a cup and saucer and I keep them in the cabinet at home as delightful reminders of our travels together.

I was only fifteen years old when I fell out with Byron. When we first split up I was heartbroken, and thought I could never live without him. But he had hurt me, and even though he came back over the following weeks to ask me to start again, I wouldn't listen. I was headstrong, and wanted to teach him a lesson – that he couldn't just behave however he liked with me. And then along came Kenny. It isn't that he was a bad man really – he was just so utterly wrapped up in his own world, a world I could never understand or enter into. He was older than me, dark and handsome, and I thought he loved me. I'd had an unsettled childhood and just wanted a happy family and a home of my own. Unlike Byron, Kenny seemed old enough to settle down. But I mistook infatuation for love, and I found out to my cost that they aren't the same thing.

It was a tough lesson to learn. But my five beautiful children brought me so many compensations, and I have their father to thank for them. I wouldn't have been without them for the world and now I believe that it was meant to be this way – my children have more than made up for the thirty years I spent living with their father.

20

THE LAST DANCE

When I look back I can hardly believe how my life panned out. It certainly wasn't how I planned it – but then, whose is? They say everyone's time on this earth is already mapped out for them and that seems to be true for me, at least.

I've been lucky with my health but after I stopped smoking, in my sixties, I started having what I called my 'funny turns'. I would suddenly feel hot, dizzy and weak, as if I'd been running, even though I was just peeling potatoes or doing the ironing. Tests showed that I had a large tumour on my left adrenal gland that needed to be removed urgently. I spent eight weeks preparing for surgery at James Cook Hospital in Middlesbrough, which had replaced the old General Hospital that held so many unhappy memories for me. The aim was to lower my blood pressure to ensure I didn't have a rush of adrenalin that could have killed me during the operation. I was lucky. To everyone's great relief the tumour turned out to be benign. When I regained consciousness after my surgery it was the first time I'd ever woken up in hospital to be greeted by the face of a loved one. Instead of the unfamiliar figure of a nurse, my lovely Byron was there waiting patiently for me to come round.

A year later I started feeling unwell again, and after more tests I was diagnosed with a blood disorder called 'polycythaemia rubra vera'. I was told the condition is normally passed down through families and is more common among Jewish people. No-one in our family had even heard of it – and we have no Jewish blood (as far as I know!). The doctors kept the condition at bay for a few years but then the treatment stopped working. To my dismay I was prescribed a low dose of a chemo-type tablet. The side effects included thinning hair – and my hair was thin enough already! The pills also wiped me out and left me feeling lethargic, but after a few months I adjusted to them.

I've always been a naturally positive person and I tried as far as possible to carry on as usual and not let my illness affect me. Byron, Julie and our lads were always there to lift my spirits and make me laugh. They encouraged me to keep active and to continue with the activities I enjoy, such as going to the theatre and walking. I even took up cycling again after Ian bought me my first ever brand-new bike for my seventieth birthday (how spoilt was I?). It was a lovely shade of cream, with a brown leather saddle. It brought to mind the time my old bike was mangled by the trolley bus when I was a little girl in North Ormesby. What I would have given to have had a shiny new bicycle back then! The years seemed to melt away as I tore along the streets around our home in Redcar – now wearing my safety helmet, of course. I even persuaded Byron to buy a bike of his own and join me, and what a sight we must have made, flying down the road together having the time of our lives and laughing as though we were a pair of kids!

On the rare occasions when Byron looked a bit grumpy in the mornings I would cheer him up with a little dance or a song.

'Come on Byron, there are plenty of people in the cemetery who would love to be still here!' I'd say. 'We have to make the most of the time we have left, because you never know...'

Well, that old saying, 'You never know what's around the corner' is so true. In August 2014 Julie was taken ill. Her job involved looking after youngsters with health issues, and at first she just thought she'd picked up a bug from one of the kids. But within a fortnight it became clear that something wasn't right and after initially being treated by the GP for Irritable Bowel Syndrome she finally went on her own initiative to James Cook Hospital, where she was diagnosed with stage three ovarian cancer.

I tried to be brave and hold my emotions in check, but inside I was screaming. I had read in one of my magazines that ovarian cancer is called the silent killer because the symptoms don't show until the disease is advanced. I could hardly believe what was happening. Julie was only fifty-three. But she was always so positive and she kept telling me not to worry. The hospital would look after her and she would fight every step of the way. But I was in turmoil – I had already lost one child and I couldn't bear losing another, I would rather die myself.

The following month, September 2014, I began to have problems with my breathing and experienced pains in my chest. I hadn't felt well for a while but I just put that down to getting older, and I was too worried about Julie and busy taking care of her to give it much thought. When I started becoming breathless, Byron and Julie urged me to go to the doctor. I was reluctant to bother him but when my condition deteriorated I finally did go.

The first doctor diagnosed a viral chest infection and told me to come back after a week if my symptoms hadn't improved. Julie was furious when I told her. She was adamant that it wasn't just a virus and insisted that I went back to the doctor's again straight away. Byron agreed and the following week he took me to see a different GP. By the time I arrived at the examination room I was completely breathless, as if I had run there, even though I had only walked from the car park outside. The doctor sent me immediately to hospital for further tests.

I was eventually told I had something called 'mesothelioma'. I didn't know what that was but I could see from poor Byron's face and the doctor's serious expression that it was bad news. This couldn't be happening now – Julie was poorly and needed me, and I needed to be with her. I was seventy-four but I didn't feel it – I was still active and people told me I seemed much younger than my years. Surely my time wasn't up already? Then I noticed that the nurse who had accompanied the doctor was holding a leaflet. On the front page I could see the title printed in white block capitals: 'COPING WITH AN END-OF-LIFE DIAGNOSIS.'

In the weeks that followed I learned that mesothelioma is an aggressive form of cancer that leads to death by respiratory failure or pneumonia. And the cause? Asbestos exposure. Of all the things that could have killed me, it would almost certainly be the tiny, hidden particles of asbestos that Kenny brought into the house on his dirty work overalls that were going to finish me off. All those years when he dumped his clothes in the cupboard for me to wash and breathe in their dust had taken their toll in more ways than one. It seems Kenny was right all along to be afraid of the contamination, and he was very successful in shielding himself from its deadly threat.

My lovely mam, who only lived to be fifty-two, had an expression for folk who reached the age of threescore years and ten – she would say that they had managed a good innings. After much soul-searching I've come to the conclusion that she was right, and I have nothing to complain about. So I'm trying my best to put on a brave face and deal with what's to come. I don't want to leave my precious family or my wonderful husband, who took me so long to find again, but I have no choice. I've decided I must make the best of the time I have left, however long that will be. I want to enjoy spending it with my family, who have always been such a source of joy to me. The hardest part is seeing the pain on the faces of Byron and my children. How I wish I could have saved them the sadness.

My beautiful family has grown over the years with the addition of wives and partners, and I am now the proud grandmother of nine grandchildren: Jolie, Christie, Eleanor, Joshua, Abbie, Katie, Bethany, Joseph and Milly. I dedicate this book to all of them.

My family. My world.

In Memory of

Joan Leech (nee Burns)
December 23rd 1940 – January 1st 2015
and
Julie McGowan
March 8th 1961 – August 11th 2021

Also Published By McGeary Media

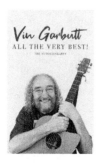

All The Very Best!
The Autobiography
by Vin Garbutt

Folk singer, guitarist, songwriter, storyteller and patter merchant, Vin Garbutt was the funniest and the most serious man on the folk scene for almost half a century.

This is Vin's touching, funny and life-affirming story in his own words.

Available in paperback and ebook from www.vingarbutt.com, Amazon and other retailers.

For updates about books from McGeary Media, sign up for the mailing list by emailing mcgearymedia@gmail.com.

Printed in Great Britain
by Amazon

15698762R00098